SIDE by SIDES

P R E S T W I C K   H O U S E ,   I N C .

OTHELLO

WILLIAM SHAKESPEARE

An abridged version

of Shakespeare's original

on the left and a

modern rendering

on the right

P.O. Box 658 • Clayton, DE 19938
Tel: 1.800.932.4593
Web site: www.prestwickhouse.com

ISBN: 1-58049-522-2

Table of Contents

DRAMATIS PERSONAE

Duke of Venice.
Brabantio, a senator.
Other Senators.
(Senator)
(First Senator)
(Second Senator)
Gratiano, brother to Brabantio.
Lodovico , kinsman to Brabantio.
Othello, a noble Moor in the service of the Venetian state.
Cassio, his lieutenant.
Iago, his ancient.
Roderigo, a Venetian gentleman.
Montano, predecessor of Othello in the government of Cyprus.

Clown, servant to Othello
Desdemona, daughter to Brabantio and wife to Othello.
Emilia, wife to Iago.
Bianca, mistress to Cassio.
Sailor
First Officer
Messenger
Gentleman
First Gentleman
Second Gentleman
Third Gentleman
First Musician

The first act takes place in Venice. The rest of the play takes place in a seaport in Cyprus.

ACT I

SCENE 1
Venice. A Street.

[Enter Roderigo and Iago]

Rod: Tush, never tell me! I take it much unkindly
    That thou, Iago, who hast had my purse
    As if the strings were thine, shouldst know of this.

Iago: 'Sblood, but you will not hear me.
5   If ever I did dream of such a matter,
    Abhor me.

Rod: Thou told'st me thou didst hold him in thy hate.

Iago: Despise me, if I do not. Three great ones of the city,
    In personal suit to make me his lieutenant,
10   Offcapp'd to him;—and, by the faith of man,
    I know my price, I am worth no worse a place:—
    But he, as loving his own pride and purposes,
    Evades them with a bombast circumstance
    Horribly stuff'd with epithets of war,
15   And, in conclusion,
    Nonsuits my mediators; for, "Certes," says he,
    "I have already chose my officer."
    And what was he?
    Forsooth, a great arithmetician,
20   One Michael Cassio, a Florentine
    A fellow almost damn'd in a fair wife[1]

[1]There is much controversary regarding interpretation of this line.

ACT I

SCENE 1
Venice. A street.

[Enter Roderigo and Iago]

ROD: *Tush! Don't tell me that! It is very upsetting that you, Iago, who I have trusted with my money as if it was yours, would do this to me.*

IAGO: *For God's sake, listen. Hate me if you think I ever imagined this.*

ROD: *You told me that you hated him.*

IAGO: *Hate me, if I do not. Three princes of the city went to him personally with a request to make me his lieutenant, tipping their hats to him. And, believe me, I know what I am worth, and I deserve the position. But Othello, being full of pride and other ideas, avoided the princes by talking pretentiously, filling his speech with references to war. In conclusion, he dismissed my supporters by saying, "I have already chosen my officer." And who was it? In truth, a great theorist, Michael Cassio, a Florentine, a man with a beautiful wife and all the trouble that goes along with that, a man who has never commanded men on a battlefield or dealt with the conflicts of war. He knows no more about war than any old lady; unless it is about the theory of battle you read in books. The senators in togas know as much about war as he does. His military skill is all talk and no action. But Cassio was chosen, and I,— whom Othello has seen with his own eyes in battle at Rhodes, at Cyprus and on other grounds, Christian and heathen,—must be like a ship on a calm sea next to a theorist. This coin-counter will be his Lieutenant soon enough and I—God bless it!—Othello's ensign.*

That never set a squadron in the field,
Nor the division of a battle knows
More than a spinster; unless the bookish theoric,
25   Wherein the toga'd consuls can propose
As masterly as he; mere prattle without practice,
Is all his soldiership. But he, sir, had the election;
And I,—of whom his eyes had seen the proof
At Rhodes, at Cyprus, and on other grounds
30   Christian and heathen,—must be belee'd and calm'd
By debitor and creditor. This countercaster,
He, in good time, must his lieutenant be,
And I—God bless the mark!—his Moorship's Ancient.

Rod: By heaven, I rather would have been his hangman.

35 Iago: Why, there's no remedy. 'Tis the curse of service,
Preferment goes by letter and affection,
And not by old gradation, where each second
Stood heir to the first. Now, sir, be judge yourself
Whether I in any just term am affined
40   To love the Moor.

Rod: I would not follow him then.

Iago: O, sir, content you.
I follow him to serve my turn upon him:
We cannot all be masters, nor all masters
45   Cannot be truly follow'd. You shall mark
Many a duteous and kneecrooking knave,
That doting on his own obsequious bondage
Wears out his time, much like his master's ass,
For naught but provender; and, when he's old, cashier'd.
50   Whip me such honest knaves. Others there are,
Who, trimm'd in forms and visages of duty,
Keep yet their hearts attending on themselves,
And throwing but shows of service on their lords
Do well thrive by them; and when they have lined their coats

ROD: *I swear I would rather be Othello's hangman.*

IAGO: *Well, there is no way around it. It is the curse of being in the armed serv-*
        ice. You get promoted by being well liked, not by seniority, where each sec-
        ond was automatically promoted to the first. Now, sir, you be the judge,
        whether I am bound by honor to love the Moor.

ROD: *I would not serve him then.*

IAGO: *Oh, sir, hold on. I follow him to get revenge on him. We cannot all be*
        masters, and all masters cannot be truly followed. You will see many loyal
        and humble servants that love to be humiliated. They work all their lives
        like mules for nothing but food, and when they get old, they are dismissed.
        I'd whip such honest fools. Others seem loyal but remember to look out
        for themselves. And by appearing to be loyal, they serve their lords well.
        These men are successful and, when they have saved up some money, they
        treat themselves very well. These fellows have some motivation, and I think
        I am one myself. For, sir, it is as sure as you are Roderigo, if I were the Moor,
        I would not be Iago. In serving him, I am only serving myself. Heaven is my
        judge, I do not serve him for love and duty, but I will appear to, for my own
        purposes. When my outward action seems to demonstrate a loyal and lov-
        ing heart, you will quickly realize that I am wearing my heart on my sleeve
        for crows to peck at. I am not what I seem to be.

55 Do themselves homage. These fellows have some soul,
  And such a one do I profess myself.
  For, sir,
  It is as sure as you are Roderigo,
  Were I the Moor, I would not be Iago.
60 In following him, I follow but myself;
  Heaven is my judge, not I for love and duty,
  But seeming so, for my peculiar end.
  For when my outward action doth demonstrate
  The native act and figure of my heart
65 In complement extern, 'tis not long after
  But I will wear my heart upon my sleeve
  For daws to peck at: I am not what I am.

ROD: *[Aside]* What a full fortune does the thicklips owe,
  If he can carry't thus!

70 IAGO: Call up her father,
  Rouse him:—make after him, poison his delight,
  Proclaim him in the streets, incense her kinsmen,
  And, though he in a fertile climate dwell,
  Plague him with flies. Though that his joy be joy,
75 Yet throw such changes of vexation on't
  As it may lose some color.

ROD: Here is her father's house; I'll call aloud.

IAGO: Do; with like timorous accent and dire yell
  As when, by night and negligence, the fire
80 Is spied in populous cities.

ROD: What, ho, Brabantio! Signior Brabantio, ho!

IAGO: Awake! What, ho, Brabantio! thieves! thieves! thieves!
  Look to your house, your daughter, and your bags!
  Thieves! thieves!

ROD: [Aside] *What an interesting future Othello has if Iago can pull this off!*

IAGO: *Call out to Desdemona's father. Wake him up, stay after him and make him miserable, denounce him in the streets, and make Desdemona's cousins angry. And even though the father is fortunate, plague him with flies and create troubles around the things he now enjoys.*

ROD: *Here is her father's house; I'll yell to him.*

IAGO: *Do it and make your yell sound both frightened and serious like how people yell when a fire is spotted in a crowded city at night.*

ROD: *What, ho, Brabantio! Signior Brabantio, ho!*

IAGO: *Awake! What, ho, Brabantio! Thieves! Thieves! Thieves! Protect your house, your daughter, and your bags! Thieves! Thieves!*

[Brabantio appears above, at a window.]

85 BRAB: What is the reason of this terrible summons?
     What is the matter there?

ROD: Signior, is all your family within?

IAGO: Are your doors lock'd?

BRAB: Why? Wherefore ask you this?

90 IAGO: 'Zounds, sir, you're robb'd! For shame, put on your gown;
     Your heart is burst, you have lost half your soul;
     Even now, now, very now, an old black ram
     Is tupping your white ewe. Arise, arise!
     Awake the snorting citizens with the bell,
95   Or else the devil will make a grandsire of you.
     Arise, I say!

BRAB: What, have you lost your wits?

ROD: Most reverend signior, do you know my voice?

BRAB: Not I. What are you?

100 ROD: My name is Roderigo.

BRAB: The worser welcome.
     I have charged thee not to haunt about my doors:
     In honest plainness thou hast heard me say
     My daughter is not for thee; and now, in madness,—
105 Being full of supper and distempering draughts,—
     Upon malicious bravery, dost thou come
     To start my quiet.

ROD: Sir, sir, sir —

[Brabantio appears above, at a window]

BRAB: *Why are you calling to me in this terrible way? What is the matter here?*

ROD: *Sir, is all your family inside?*

IAGO: *Are your doors locked?*

BRAB: *Why do you ask this?*

IAGO: *I swear, sir, you have been robbed. For shame, get dressed. Your heart is broken, you have lost half your soul. As we speak, an old black ram is mating with your white ewe. Get up, get up! Wake the snoring citizens with the bell, or else the devil will make a grandfather out of you. Get up, I say!*

BRAB: *What, have you lost your mind?*

ROD: *Most reverend sir, do you know my voice?*

BRAB: *No, I do not. Who are you?*

ROD: *My name is Roderigo.*

BRAB: *I am not glad to see you. I have asked you not to hang around here. I have honestly and clearly told you that my daughter is not for you. And now, in some kind of drunken madness, with malicious recklessness, you come to wake me up.*

ROD: *Sir, sir, sir—*

BRAB: But thou must needs be sure
110   My spirit and my place have in them power
       To make this bitter to thee.

ROD: Patience, good sir.

BRAB: What tell'st thou me of robbing? This is Venice;
       My house is not a grange.

115 ROD: Most grave Brabantio,
       In simple and pure soul I come to you.

IAGO: 'Zounds, sir, you are one of those that will not serve God, if the
       devil bid you. Because we come to do you service and you think
       we are ruffians, you'll have your daughter covered with a Barbary
120   horse; you'll have your nephews neigh to you; you'll have coursers
       for cousins, and gennets for germans.

BRAB: What profane wretch art thou?

IAGO: I am one, sir, that comes to tell you your daughter and the Moor
       are now making the beast with two backs.

125 BRAB: Thou art a villain.

IAGO: You are—a senator.

BRAB: This thou shalt answer; I know thee, Roderigo.

ROD: Sir, I will answer any thing. But, I beseech you,
       If't be your pleasure and most wise consent,
130   As partly I find it is, that your fair daughter,
       At this odd-even and dull watch o' the night,
       Transported, with no worse nor better guard
       But with a knave of common hire, a gondolier,
       To the gross clasps of a lascivious Moor—
135   If this be known to you, and your allowance,

14

BRAB: But you can be sure that I have the power to make this a difficult place for you to live.

ROD: Patience, good sir.

BRAB: What is all this about robbery? This is Venice. My house is not a farm-house.

ROD: Most serious Brabantio, I come to you a simple and honest man.

IAGO: Good lord, sir, you are one of those who will not serve god if the devil tells you to do it. Because we come to do you a favor and you think that we are hoodlums, you'll let your daughter be mounted by an African horse. You'll have your nephews neigh to you, and you'll have stallions for cousins, and little horses for grandchildren

BRAB: What kind of offensive wretch are you?

IAGO: I am the kind, sir, that has come to tell you that your daughter is in bed with the Moor.

BRAB: You are a villain.

IAGO: You are [Thinking better of what he was going to say]—a senator.

BRAB: You will answer this question. I know you, Roderigo.

ROD: Sir, I will answer anything. But, I beg you, please listen. If you want your fair daughter to be taken, with no more of a chaperone than a common boat-man, into the lusty arms of Othello at this time of night—and if you already know this and she has your permission—then we were bold and wrong to wake you. But if you didn't know about this, then my manners tell me that you have unfairly criticized us. Do not think that, against all good manners, I would play games with you, sir. I say again that unless she has your per-mission, your daughter is rebelling. She is giving her honor, beauty, wit and

We then have done you bold and saucy wrongs;
But, if you know not this, my manners tell me
We have your wrong rebuke. Do not believe
That, from the sense of all civility,
140   I thus would play and trifle with your reverence.
Your daughter, if you have not given her leave,
I say again, hath made a gross revolt,
Tying her duty, beauty, wit, and fortunes
In an extravagant and wheeling stranger
145   Of here and everywhere. Straight satisfy yourself:
If she be in her chamber or your house,
Let loose on me the justice of the state
For thus deluding you.

BRAB: Strike on the tinder, ho!
150   Give me a taper! Call up all my people!
This accident is not unlike my dream;
Belief of it oppresses me already.
Light, I say, light!   *[Exit above]*

IAGO: Farewell, for I must leave you.
155   It seems not meet, nor wholesome to my place,
To be produced—as, if I stay, I shall—
Against the Moor; for I do know, the state,—
However this may gall him with some check,—
Cannot with safety cast him; for he's embark'd
160   With such loud reason to the Cyprus' wars,
Which even now stands in act, that, for their souls,
Another of his fathom they have none
To lead their business; in which regard,
Though I do hate him as I do hell-pains,
165   Yet for necessity of present life,
I must show out a flag and sign of love,
Which is indeed but sign. That you shall surely find him,
Lead to the Sagittary the raised search,
And there will I be with him. So farewell.   *[Exit.]*

fortunes to a stranger who roams everywhere. Satisfy yourself. If she is in her room asleep, let the law punish me for trying to delude you.

BRAB: *Light the fire, ho! Give me a candle! Call up all my people! This incident is like a dream I just had. I am already distressed about it. Light, I say! light!*   [Exit]

IAGO: [To Roderigo] *Farewell, for I must leave you. It wouldn't look right for me to stay, and be presented as a witness against the Moor, for I do know this state. And however it may bother Othello to be questioned by Brabantio and reprimanded, he is urgently headed for the wars of Cyprus, which are raging even now. The state does not have another general as good as him to lead them in this fight. Although I hate him as I hate the pains of hell, my situation requires that I act loyal to him—but I am only acting. You will surely find him by leading the search party to the Sagittary tavern. There I will be with him. So, farewell.*   [Exit]

[Enter Brabantio and Servants with torches.]

170 BRAB: It is too true an evil: gone she is,
And what's to come of my despised time
Is nought but bitterness.—Now, Roderigo,
Where didst thou see her? — O unhappy girl!—
With the Moor, say'st thou?—Who would be a father!
175 How didst thou know 'twas she? —O, she deceives me
Past thought!—What said she to you?—Get more tapers.
Raise all my kindred. —Are they married, think you?

ROD: Truly, I think they are.

BRAB: O heaven!—How got she out? —O treason of the blood!
180 Fathers, from hence trust not your daughters' minds
By what you see them act. Are there not charms
By which the property of youth and maidhood
May be abused? Have you not read, Roderigo,
Of some such thing?

185 ROD: Yes, sir, I have indeed.

BRAB: Call up my brother. —Do you know
Where we may apprehend her and the Moor?

ROD: I think I can discover him, if you please
To get good guard, and go along with me.

190 BRAB: Pray you, lead on. At every house I'll call;
I may command at most.—Get weapons, ho!
And raise some special officers of night.—
On, good Roderigo,—I'll deserve your pains.

[Exeunt.]

[Enter Brabantio, and Servants with torches]

BRAB: *It is an evil truth. She is gone and now my hated life will be full of nothing but bitterness. Now Roderigo, where did you see her? Oh, unhappy girl! With the Moor, you say—who intends to have a child! How did you know it was Desdemona? Oh, she deceives me so much I can't think about it! What did she say to you?* [To servant] *Get more candles. Wake my people. Do you think they are married yet?*

ROD: *Truly, I think they are.*

BRAB: *Oh, heaven! How did she get out? She has betrayed her family! Fathers, from now on do not assume that your daughters' minds reflect how you see them act. Aren't there spells that may be used to fool young maidens? Haven't you read about something like that, Roderigo?*

ROD: *Yes, sir, I have indeed.*

BRAB: *Call up my brother. Do you know where we can catch her and the Moor?*

ROD: *I think I can find him if you could get some good men and come along with me.*

BRAB: *Please, lead on. I will stop at every house. At most houses I can order men to go with me. Get weapons, and form a special posse. Let's go, good Roderigo; I will reward you for your services.*

[Exeunt]

19

SCENE 2
Another street.

[Enter Othello, Iago, and Attendants with torches.]

IAGO: Though in the trade of war I have slain men,
    Yet do I hold it very stuff o' the conscience
    To do no contrived murder. I lack iniquity
    Sometimes to do me service. Nine or ten times
5   I had thought to have yerk'd him here under the ribs.

OTHELLO: 'Tis better as it is.

IAGO: Nay, but he prated
    And spoke such scurvy and provoking terms
    Against your honor
10   That, with the little godliness I have,
    I did full hard forbear him. But I pray you, sir,
    Are you fast married? Be assured of this,
    That the magnifico is much beloved,
    And hath in his effect a voice potential
15   As double as the Duke's. He will divorce you,
    Or put upon you what restraint and grievance
    The law, with all his might to enforce it on,
    Will give him cable.

OTHELLO: Let him do his spite.
20   My services, which I have done the signiory,
    Shall out-tongue his complaints. 'Tis yet to know—
    Which, when I know that boasting is an honor,
    I shall promulgate—I fetch my life and being
    From men of royal siege; and my demerits
25   May speak unbonneted to as proud a fortune
    As this that I have reach'd. For know, Iago,
    But that I love the gentle Desdemona,
    I would not my unhoused free condition
    Put into circumscription and confine
30   For the sea's worth. But, look! What lights come yond?

20

SCENE 2
Another street.

[Enter Othello, Iago, and Attendants with torches]

IAGO: *Although I have slain men in war, I still have a conscience and lack the evil required to commit a premeditated murder. Nine or ten times I have thought about stabbing Roderigo, here under the ribs.*

OTHELLO: *It is better that you did not.*

IAGO: *No, but he boasted and said such insulting things about your lack of honor that it took all of the goodness I have to stand it. But, I ask you, sir, are you securely married? Believe me that Brabantio is well liked, and his voice is possibly twice as powerful as the Duke's. He will have you divorced, or with all his might, he will cause whatever restriction and suffering he can to you under the law.*

OTHELLO: *Let him do his best. My services to the city are worth more than his complaints. He doesn't know it yet, and I won't boast about it until the right time, but I, too, come from royal blood. My good qualities will show that I come from as fine a fortune as the one that I have married into. Know, Iago, that I love the gentle Desdemona; otherwise, I would not have given up my freedom and put myself into the prison of marriage for all the money in the world. But look, what lights are those coming up?*

IAGO: Those are the raised father and his friends.
    You were best go in.

OTHELLO: Not I; I must be found.
    My parts, my title, and my perfect soul
35   Shall manifest me rightly. Is it they?

IAGO: By Janus, I think no.

[Enter Cassio and certain Officers with torches.]

OTHELLO: The servants of the Duke?
    And my lieutenant?
    The goodness of the night upon you, friends!
40   What is the news?

CASSIO: The Duke does greet you, general,
    And he requires your haste-post-haste appearance,
    Even on the instant.

OTHELLO: What is the matter, think you?

45   CASSIO: Something from Cyprus, as I may divine;
    It is a business of some heat. The galleys
    Have sent a dozen sequent messengers
    This very night at one another's heels;
    And many of the consuls, raised and met,
50   Are at the Duke's already. You have been hotly call'd for;
    When, being not at your lodging to be found,
    The Senate hath sent about three quests
    To search you out.

OTHELLO: 'Tis well I am found by you.
55   I will but spend a word here in the house
    And go with you.   *[Exit.]*

CASSIO: Ancient, what makes he here?

22

IAGO: *Those are her awakened father and his friends. You had better go in.*

OTHELLO: *Not I. I will be found. My presence, my title, and my perfect soul will show what I really am. Is it they?*

IAGO: *By Janus, I don't think so.*

[Enter Cassio, and Officers with torches]

OTHELLO: *The servants of the Duke and my lieutenant? Good evening to you, friends! What is the news?*

CASSIO: *The Duke sends his greeting to you, general. He needs to see you immediately. At once!*

OTHELLO: *What is the matter, do you think?*

CASSIO: *Something from Cyprus, I believe. It is a business of some importance. The warships have sent a dozen messengers tonight, one right after the other. Many of the council members have been awakened and are at the Duke's already. You have been urgently called for. When you were not found at your apartment, the Senate sent three people to search for you.*

OTHELLO: *It is good you found me. I will tell them in the house, and then I'll go with you.* [Exit]

CASSIO: *Ensign, why is Othello here?*

IAGO: Faith, he tonight hath boarded a land carack;
If it prove lawful prize, he's made forever.

60   CASSIO: I do not understand.

IAGO: He's married.

CASSIO: To who?

[Reenter Othello.]

IAGO: Marry, to—Come, captain, will you go?

OTHELLO: Have with you.

65   CASSIO: Here comes another troop to seek for you.

IAGO: It is Brabantio.—General, be advised;
He comes to bad intent.

[Enter Brabantio, Roderigo, and Officers with torches and weapons.]

OTHELLO: Holla! Stand there!

ROD: Signior, it is the Moor.

70   BRAB: Down with him, thief!   *[They draw on both sides.]*

IAGO: You, Roderigo! Come, sir, I am for you.

OTHELLO: Keep up your bright swords, for the dew will rust them.—
Good signior, you shall more command with years
Than with your weapons.

75   BRAB: O thou foul thief, where hast thou stow'd my daughter?
Damn'd as thou art, thou hast enchanted her,

24

IAGO: *Tonight he has taken over a wealthy caravan. If it remains his lawful prize, he is set for life.*

CASSIO: *I do not understand.*

IAGO: [Whispering] *He's married.*

CASSIO: *To whom?*

[Reenter Othello]

IAGO: *By Mary, to*—[Not wanting to be caught talking behind Othello's back] *Come, captain, will you go?*

OTHELLO: *I am ready.*

CASSIO: *Here comes another group looking for you.*

IAGO: *It is Brabantio. General, be advised, he comes with bad intentions.*

[Enter Brabantio, Roderigo, and Officers with torches and weapons]

OTHELLO: *Hello! Stand there!*

ROD: *Sir, it is the Moor.*

BRAB: *Take the thief down!*   [Both sides draw weapons]

IAGO: *You, Roderigo! Come, sir, I will fight you.*

OTHELLO: *Put away your shiny swords, or the dew will rust them. Good sir, you have more authority over me by your age than because of your weapons.*

BRAB: *Oh, you foul thief, where have you hidden my daughter? Damned as you are, you have enchanted her. I will use logic to prove my point. If she was not bound in chains of magic, why would a maid so tender, fair, and*

25

For I'll refer me to all things of sense,
If she in chains of magic were not bound,
Whether a maid so tender, fair, and happy,
80   So opposite to marriage that she shunn'd
The wealthy, curled darlings of our nation,
Would ever have, to incur a general mock,
Run from her guardage to the sooty bosom
Of such a thing as thou—to fear, not to delight.
85   Judge me the world, if 'tis not gross in sense
That thou hast practiced on her with foul charms;
Abused her delicate youth with drugs or minerals
That weaken motion:—I'll have't disputed on;
'Tis probable, and palpable to thinking.
90   I therefore apprehend and do attach thee
For an abuser of the world, a practicer
Of arts inhibited and out of warrant.—
Lay hold upon him. If he do resist,
Subdue him at his peril.

95   OTHELLO: Hold your hands,
Both you of my inclining, and the rest:
Were it my cue to fight, I should have known it
Without a prompter.—Where will you that I go
To answer this your charge?

95   BRAB: To prison; till fit time
Of law and course of direct session,
Call thee to answer.

OTHELLO: What if I do obey?
How may the Duke be therewith satisfied,
100   Whose messengers are here about my side,
Upon some present business of the state
To bring me to him?

FIRST OFFICER: 'Tis true, most worthy signior;
The Duke's in council, and your noble self,
105   I am sure, is sent for.

26

happy—so opposed to marriage that she shunned the wealthy, handsome men of our nation—have run from her protection to the dark bosom of such a thing as you, knowing she'd be ridiculed. This is something to fear, not to delight in. Let the world decide if it makes sense. You have practiced some evil magic on her and taken advantage of her delicate youth with drugs or minerals that weaken the mind. I will let the courts decide. It is the proper thing to do. Therefore, I arrest you and charge you with being a sorcerer, an abuser of the world, a practitioner of illegal magical arts. Seize him. If he resists, subdue him at his peril.

OTHELLO: Put your hands down, all of you. If it were time to fight, I would know it without having to be told. Where do you wish me to go to answer your charge?

BRAB: To prison until you are called to answer this case in court.

OTHELLO: What if I obey? What would the Duke think? Have his messengers, who are here by my side, been sent on some urgent business of the state to bring me to him?

FIRST OFFICER: It is true, most worthy sir. The Duke is in council, and I am sure that your noble self has been sent for.

BRAB: How? The Duke in council?
In this time of the night?—Bring him away;
Mine's not an idle cause. The Duke himself,
Or any of my brothers of the state,
110   Cannot but feel this wrong as 'twere their own;
For if such actions may have passage free,
Bond-slaves and pagans shall our statesmen be.

[Exeunt.]

SCENE 3

A council chamber.
The Duke and Senators sitting at a table; Officers attending.

DUKE: There is no composition in these news
That gives them credit.

FIRST SENATOR. Indeed they are disproportion'd;
My letters say a hundred and seven galleys.

5   DUKE: And mine, a hundred and forty.

SECOND SENATOR: And mine, two hundred.
But though they jump not on a just account—
As in these cases, where the aim reports,
'Tis oft with difference—yet do they all confirm
10   A Turkish fleet, and bearing up to Cyprus.

DUKE: Nay, it is possible enough to judgement:
I do not so secure me in the error,
But the main article I do approve
In fearful sense.

15   SAILOR: *[Within.]* What, ho! What, ho! What, ho!

FIRST OFFICER: A messenger from the galleys.

28

BRAB: *What? The Duke in council? At this time of night? Bring Othello anyway; my cause is important enough. The Duke himself, or any of my brothers in the council, will feel that this is a wrong committed against them too, because if such actions are not punished, slaves and pagans will become our statesmen.*

[Exeunt]

SCENE 3

A council chamber.
The Duke and Senators are sitting at a table with Officers attending.

DUKE: *There is no consistency in these reports to give them credibility.*

FIRST SENATOR: *Indeed, different numbers are being reported. My reports say one hundred and seven warships.*

DUKE: *And mine, a hundred and forty.*

SECOND SENATOR: *And mine, two hundred. But even though the numbers vary—in this kind of situation, there are often differences—they all confirm that a Turkish fleet is heading toward Cyprus.*

DUKE: *This is enough information to form a judgment. I am not comforted by the error, but I am afraid I do agree on the main point.*

SAILOR: [Off stage] *What, ho! What, ho! What, ho!*

FIRST OFFICER: *A messenger has come from the ships.*

[Enter Sailor.]

DUKE: Now, what's the business?

SAILOR: The Turkish preparation makes for Rhodes;
   So was I bid report here to the state
20   By Signior Angelo.

DUKE: How say you by this change?

FIRST SENATOR: This cannot be,
   By no assay of reason; 'tis a pageant
   To keep us in false gaze. When we consider
25   The importancy of Cyprus to the Turk;
   And let ourselves again but understand
   That as it more concerns the Turk than Rhodes,
   So may he with more facile question bear it,
   For that it stands not in such warlike brace,
30   But altogether lacks the abilities
   That Rhodes is dress'd in;—
   If we make thought of this,
   We must not think the Turk is so unskillful
   To leave that latest which concerns him first,
35   Neglecting an attempt of ease and gain,
   To wake and wage a danger profitless.

DUKE: Nay, in all confidence, he's not for Rhodes.

FIRST OFFICER: Here is more news.

[Enter a Messenger.]

MESSENGER: The Ottomites, reverend and gracious,
40   Steering with due course toward the isle of Rhodes,
   Have there injointed them with an after fleet.

FIRST SENATOR: Ay, so I thought. How many, as you guess?

[Enter a Sailor]

DUKE: *Now, what's the situation?*

SAILOR: *The Turkish troops are heading for Rhodes. I was told to report the news here by Signior Angelo.*

DUKE: *What do you say about this change?*

FIRST SENATOR: *This cannot be. It does not make sense. It is a diversion to make us look away from the main target. When we consider the importance of Cyprus to the Turks—and remember that Cyprus is not only more important to the Turks than Rhodes is, but it is also less heavily defended. We must not think that the Turks are so foolish as to ignore Cyprus, which is more important to them and could be captured easily, in order to attempt a more difficult attack that would benefit them less.*

DUKE: *No, in all confidence, the Turks are not headed for Rhodes.*

FIRST OFFICER: *Here is more news.*

[Enter a Messenger]

MESSENGER: *Reverent and gracious sir, the Ottoman Turks, which were steering toward the isle of Rhodes, have joined with a second fleet.*

FIRST SENATOR: *Yes, I thought so. How many, would you guess?*

MESSENGER: Of thirty sail; and now they do restem
    Their backward course, bearing with frank appearance
45   Their purposes toward Cyprus. Signior Montano,
    Your trusty and most valiant servitor,
    With his free duty recommends you thus,
    And prays you to believe him.

DUKE: 'Tis certain then for Cyprus.
50   Marcus Luccicos, is not he in town?

FIRST SENATOR: He's now in Florence.

DUKE: Write from us to him, postposthaste dispatch.

FIRST SENATOR: Here comes Brabantio and the valiant Moor.

[Enter Brabantio, Othello, Iago, Roderigo, and Officers.]

DUKE: Valiant Othello, we must straight employ you
55   Against the general enemy Ottoman.
    [To Brabantio] I did not see you; welcome, gentle signior;
    We lack'd your counsel and your help tonight.

BRAB: So did I yours. Good your Grace, pardon me:
    Neither my place nor aught I heard of business
60   Hath raised me from my bed, nor doth the general care
    Take hold on me; for my particular grief
    Is of so floodgate and o'erbearing nature
    That it engluts and swallows other sorrows,
    And it is still itself.

65   DUKE: Why, what's the matter?

BRAB: My daughter! O, my daughter!

ALL: Dead?

MESSENGER: *Thirty ships; having joined up, they have turned and are retracing their course, heading openly and boldly toward Cyprus. Signior Montano, your trusty and most valiant servant has sent this message and prays that you believe him.*

DUKE: *'Tis certain then; the Turks are headed for Cyprus. Is Marcus Luccicos in town?*

FIRST SENATOR: *He's now in Florence.*

DUKE: *Write him an urgent dispatch.*

FIRST SENATOR: *Here comes Brabantio and the valiant Moor.*

[Enter Brabantio, Othello, Iago, Roderigo, and Officers]

DUKE: *Valiant Othello, we must send you right away to fight the enemy Ottoman Turk.* [To Brabantio] *I did not see you; welcome, gentle sir. We lacked your counsel and your help tonight.*

BRAB: *I also missed yours. Your good grace, pardon me while I explain: The business before the state has not raised me from my bed for I had not heard of it. The general crisis does not concern me because my personal grief is so great that it floods over and swallows other sorrows, and it is still itself.*

DUKE: *Why, what's the matter?*

BRAB: *My daughter! Oh, my daughter!*

ALL: *Dead?*

33

BRAB: Ay, to me.
    She is abused, stol'n from me and corrupted
70   By spells and medicines bought of mountebanks;
    For nature so preposterously to err,
    Being not deficient, blind, or lame of sense,
    Sans witchcraft could not.

DUKE: Whoe'er he be that in this foul proceeding
75   Hath thus beguiled your daughter of herself
    And you of her, the bloody book of law
    You shall yourself read in the bitter letter
    After your own sense.

BRAB: Humbly I thank your Grace.
80   Here is the man, this Moor; whom now, it seems,
    Your special mandate for the state affairs
    Hath hither brought.

ALL: We are very sorry for't.

DUKE: *[To Othello]* What in your own part can you say to this?

85 BRAB: Nothing, but this is so.

OTHELLO: Most potent, grave, and reverend signiors,
    My very noble and approved good masters,
    That I have ta'en away this old man's daughter,
    It is most true; true, I have married her;
90   The very head and front of my offending
    Hath this extent, no more. Rude am I in my speech,
    And little blest with the soft phrase of peace;
    For since these arms of mine had seven years' pith,
    Till now some nine moons wasted, they have used
95   Their dearest action in the tented field,
    And little of this great world can I speak,
    More than pertains to feats of broil and battle;
    And therefore little shall I grace my cause

BRAB: Yes, to me she is. She has been fooled, stolen from me, and corrupted by spells and medicines bought from cheating salesmen. She is not mentally impaired, blind, or senseless, so there is no way this could have happened without witchcraft.

DUKE: Whoever has disgustingly tricked your daughter and stolen her from you will be dealt with through the bloody book of the law. You will read the punishment based on your own judgment.

BRAB: Humbly, I thank your grace. Here is the man. This Moor, it seems, has been brought to you by your own special order.

ALL: We are very sorry for that.

DUKE: [To Othello] What can you say about this on your own behalf?

BRAB: Nothing, except that it is true.

OTHELLO: Most powerful, grave, and esteemed sirs, my noble and proven good masters, it is true that I have taken away this old man's daughter. I have married her. That is my offense, from top to bottom, and no more than that. I have common and rough speech, and I am not blessed with a soothing way of speaking. Until nine months ago, I have used my voice only in battle for nearly seven years. I can speak little of this great world except that which pertains to feats of battle. Therefore, I shall not help my cause by speaking for myself. Yet by your gracious patience, I will tell a candid tale of the course of my love–a story about what drugs, what charms, what spells, and what mighty magic I am charged with using to win his daughter.

In speaking for myself. Yet, by your gracious patience,
100   I will a round unvarnish'd tale deliver
Of my whole course of love: what drugs, what charms,
What conjuration, and what mighty magic
For such proceeding I am charged withal
I won his daughter.

105 BRAB: A maiden never bold;
Of spirit so still and quiet that her motion
Blush'd at herself; and she—in spite of nature,
Of years, of country, credit, everything—
To fall in love with what she fear'd to look on!
110   It is judgement maim'd and most imperfect,
That will confess perfection so could err
Against all rules of nature, I therefore vouch again,
That with some mixtures powerful o'er the blood,
Or with some dram conjured to this effect,
115   He wrought upon her.

DUKE: To vouch this, is no proof,
Without more certain and more overt test
Than these thin habits and poor likelihoods
Of modern seeming do prefer against him.

120 FIRST SENATOR: But, Othello, speak.
Did you by indirect and forced courses
Subdue and poison this young maid's affections?
Or came it by request, and such fair question
As soul to soul affordeth?

125 OTHELLO: I do beseech you,
Send for the lady to the Sagittary,
And let her speak of me before her father:
If you do find me foul in her report,
The trust, the office I do hold of you,
130   Not only take away, but let your sentence
Even fall upon my life.

BRAB: A shy maiden with such a still and quiet temperament: How could she, in spite of her nature, of her years, her country, everything—fall in love with what she feared to look at! It is a very flawed judgment that could believe such perfection could go against all rules of nature. I, therefore, say again that with some powerful mixtures, or with some potion fashioned to this effect, he overcame her blood and worked his will upon her.

DUKE: Just saying this is not proof. We need a more certain and more conclusive test than these unlikely and common statements brought against him.

FIRST SENATOR: But, Othello, speak. Did you subdue and poison this young maid's love by devious and unnatural actions? Or did you ask for her love in the tender way that a soul uses to find another soul?

OTHELLO: I beg you, to send for Desdemona at the Sagittary and let her speak about me in front of her father. If you find me to be evil according to her, take away the trust that you have in me, the office that you have given me, and even take away my life.

DUKE: Fetch Desdemona hither.

OTHELLO: Ancient, conduct them; you best know the place.

[Exeunt Iago and Attendants.]

And till she come, as truly as to heaven

135   I do confess the vices of my blood,

So justly to your grave ears I'll present

How I did thrive in this fair lady's love

And she in mine.

DUKE: Say it, Othello.

140 OTHELLO: Her father loved me, oft invited me,

Still question'd me the story of my life

From year to year, the battles, sieges, fortunes,

That I have pass'd.

I ran it through, even from my boyish days

145   To the very moment that he bade me tell it:

Wherein I spake of most disastrous chances,

Of moving accidents by flood and field,

Of hairbreadth 'scapes i' the imminent deadly breach,

Of being taken by the insolent foe,

150   And sold to slavery, of my redemption thence,

And portance in my travels' history;

Wherein of antres vast and deserts idle,

Rough quarries, rocks, and hills whose heads touch heaven,

It was my hint to speak,— such was the process;

155   And of the Cannibals that each other eat,

The Anthropophagi, and men whose heads

Do grow beneath their shoulders. This to hear

Would Desdemona seriously incline;

But still the house affairs would draw her thence,

160   Which ever as she could with haste dispatch,

She'ld come again, and with a greedy ear

Devour up my discourse; which I observing,

Took once a pliant hour, and found good means

To draw from her a prayer of earnest heart

165   That I would all my pilgrimage dilate,

DUKE: *Bring Desdemona here.*

OTHELLO: *Ensign, show them to the Sagittary. You know the place best.*
[Exit Iago and Attendants]
And until she arrives, I will confess my feelings to you as if I were telling God. I'll tell about how she came to love me and I came to love her.

DUKE: *Tell me, Othello.*

OTHELLO: *Her father loved me and often invited me to his house to tell him stories about my life. I recounted, year by year, the battles, sieges, and fortunes that I was involved in. I told him everything, from my boyhood days to the very moment that he asked me tell about my adventures. I spoke of all disastrous fortune: events on the seas and the battlefield, narrow escapes, and the turning points of battles. I also told about being taken by a terrible enemy and sold into slavery. I spoke of my release and my travels when I had to pass through caves and vast deserts alone, through rough quarries, over rocks, and mountains reaching heaven. It went that way. And I would tell him about the cannibals who ate each other, the man-eaters, and about men whose heads grow beneath their shoulders. Although Desdemona would attempt to hear these stories, affairs of the house would take her away. But whenever she could finish quickly, she would come back again, and take in my stories with an eager ear. I saw that she was interested, and once in an hour, I found a way to get her to earnestly ask me to relate all my adventures to her, most of which she had heard only in part. I agreed. She often cried when I spoke of some distressful situation that I suffered through when I was young. When my story was done, she gave me many sighs for my trouble. She swore, honestly, that it was strange, extremely strange. She said, "'Twas pitiful, 'twas wondrous pitiful." She wished she had not heard; yet she wished that heaven had made her that kind of a man. She thanked me and told me that if I had a friend who loved her, I should teach him only how to tell my story, because that would win her heart. When she gave this hint, I spoke up. She loved me for the dangers I had encountered, and I loved her because she pitied them. This is the only witchcraft I have used. Here comes Desdemona; let her verify what I have said.*

Whereof by parcels she had something heard,
But not intentively. I did consent,
And often did beguile her of her tears
When I did speak of some distressful stroke
170 That my youth suffer'd. My story being done,
She gave me for my pains a world of sighs;
She swore, in faith, 'twas strange, 'twas passing strange;
'Twas pitiful, 'twas wondrous pitiful.
She wish'd she had not heard it, yet she wish'd
175 That heaven had made her such a man; she thank'd me,
And bade me, if I had a friend that loved her,
I should but teach him how to tell my story,
And that would woo her. Upon this hint I spake:
She loved me for the dangers I had pass'd,
180 And I loved her that she did pity them.
This only is the witchcraft I have used.
Here comes the lady; let her witness it.

[Enter Desdemona, Iago, and Attendants.]

DUKE: I think this tale would win my daughter too.
Good Brabantio,
185 Take up this mangled matter at the best:
Men do their broken weapons rather use
Than their bare hands.

BRAB: I pray you, hear her speak:
If she confess that she was half the wooer,
190 Destruction on my head, if my bad blame
Light on the man! Come hither, gentle mistress:
Do you perceive in all this noble company
Where most you owe obedience?

DESD: My noble father,
195 I do perceive here a divided duty.
To you I am bound for life and education;
My life and education both do learn me
How to respect you; you are the lord of duty,

40

[Enter Desdemona, Iago, and Attendants]

DUKE: *I think this tale would win my daughter, too. Good Brabantio, make the best out of this difficult matter. Men do use their broken weapons rather than their bare hands.*

BRAB: *I beg you, hear her speak. If she confesses that she was half the seducer, let my life be destroyed because I have wrongly accused this man. Come here, gentle girl. To whom among this noble group do you owe the most obedience and respect?*

DESD: *My noble father, I see here a divided duty. I am bound to honor you for my life and education. My life and education both teach me to respect you. You are the lord of duty, and I am here as your daughter. But here is my husband, and as much respect as my mother showed to you by choosing you over her father, I suggest that is what I owe to my lord, the Moor.*

I am hitherto your daughter. But here's my husband,
200   And so much duty as my mother show'd
To you, preferring you before her father,
So much I challenge that I may profess
Due to the Moor, my lord.

BRAB: God be with you! I have done.
205   Please it your Grace, on to the state affairs;
I had rather to adopt a child than get it.
Come hither, Moor:
I here do give thee that with all my heart
Which, but thou hast already, with all my heart
210   I would keep from thee. For your sake, jewel,
I am glad at soul I have no other child;
For thy escape would teach me tyranny,
To hang clogs on them. I have done, my lord.

DUKE: Let me speak like yourself, and lay a sentence
215   Which, as a grise or step, may help these lovers
Into your favor.
When remedies are past, the griefs are ended
By seeing the worst, which late on hopes depended.
To mourn a mischief that is past and gone
220   Is the next way to draw new mischief on.
What cannot be preserved when fortune takes,
Patience her injury a mockery makes.
The robb'd that smiles steals something from the thief;
He robs himself that spends a bootless grief.

225 BRAB: So let the Turk of Cyprus us beguile;
We lose it not so long as we can smile.
He bears the sentence well, that nothing bears
But the free comfort which from thence he hears;
But he bears both the sentence and the sorrow
230   That, to pay grief, must of poor patience borrow.
These sentences, to sugar or to gall,
Being strong on both sides, are equivocal.

42

BRAB: *God be with you! I am done. If it please your Grace, we may move on to state affairs: I would rather adopt a child than have this one. Come here, Moor. I give you, with all my heart, what you already have, and what, with all my heart, I would keep from you. For your sake, precious girl, my heart is glad that I have no other child because your escapade would teach me tyranny and I'd hang chains on them. I am done, my lord.*

DUKE: *Let me speak in your place, and pronounce a sentence which may act as a bridge or step to help you approve of these lovers again. When what you wanted can't happen, it will make you feel better to imagine the worst that could have come of your hopes. To sulk about some mischief that is past and gone is a sure way to bring more trouble. When things turn bad, and we patiently keep the past alive in our hearts, we make a joke of the injury. When the man being robbed smiles, he steals something from the thief. The man who indulges in a long and useless grief only robs himself.*

BRAB: *So let the Turk rob us of Cyprus. We don't really lose it as long as we can be cheerful. You manage the punishment well, if you take nothing from it but free advice, but he who pays the sentence with his grief and sorrow must use patience. The meaning of these words, either sweet or bitter, is uncertain. But words are words; I never heard of a heart being broken solely by hearing words. I humbly ask you to tell me about the affairs of state.*

43

But words are words; I never yet did hear
That the bruised heart was pierced through the ear.
235 I humbly beseech you, proceed to the affairs of state.

DUKE: The Turk with a most mighty preparation makes for Cyprus.
Othello, the fortitude of the place is best known to you; and though
we have there a substitute of most allowed sufficiency, yet opinion,
a sovereign mistress of effects, throws a more safer voice on you.
240 You must therefore be content to slubber the gloss of your new fortunes with this more stubborn and boisterous expedition.

OTHELLO: The tyrant custom, most grave senators,
Hath made the flinty and steel couch of war
My thrice driven bed of down. I do agnize
245 A natural and prompt alacrity
I find in hardness and do undertake
These present wars against the Ottomites.
Most humbly therefore bending to your state,
I crave fit disposition for my wife,
250 Due reference of place and exhibition,
With such accommodation and besort
As levels with her breeding.

DUKE: If you please,
Be't at her father's.

255 BRAB: I'll not have it so.

OTHELLO: Nor I.

DESD: Nor I. I would not there reside
To put my father in impatient thoughts
By being in his eye. Most gracious Duke,
260 To my unfolding lend your prosperous ear.

DUKE: What would you, Desdemona?

44

DUKE: The Turk is heading for Cyprus with a strong force. Othello, you know the defenses of Cyprus the best, and although we have a competent substitute for you in place, most people think it would be better if you were there. You must, therefore, delay the happiness of your new marriage until after this mission is completed.

OTHELLO: My fate, somber Senators, is to be a soldier. Three times has war made my featherbed one of steel and stone. I am happily ready to face difficult circumstances. I will quickly undertake the wars against the Turks. However, bowing to your office, I need to know that someone is taking care of my wife, in a manner that her station in society and breeding require.

DUKE: If it is fine with you, she can stay with her father.

BRAB: I will not allow that.

OTHELLO: Nor will I.

DESD: Nor will I. I would not want to stay there and make my father uncomfortable. Most gracious Duke, please listen to my request.

DUKE: What do you want to do, Desdemona?

DESD: That I did love the Moor to live with him,
My downright violence and storm of fortunes
May trumpet to the world. My heart's subdued
Even to the very quality of my lord:
265   I saw Othello's visage in his mind,
And to his honors and his valiant parts
Did I my soul and fortunes consecrate.
So that, dear lords, if I be left behind,
A moth of peace, and he go to the war,
270   The rites for which I love him are bereft me,
And I a heavy interim shall support
By his dear absence. Let me go with him.

OTHELLO: Let her have your voices.
Vouch with me, heaven, I therefore beg it not
275   To please the palate of my appetite;
Nor to comply with heat the young affects
In me defunct—and proper satisfaction;
But to be free and bounteous to her mind;
And heaven defend your good souls, that you think
280   I will your serious and great business scant
For she is with me. No, when lightwing'd toys
Of feather'd Cupid seel with wanton dullness
My speculative and officed instruments,
That my disports corrupt and taint my business,
285   Let housewives make a skillet of my helm,
And all indign and base adversities
Make head against my estimation!

DUKE: Be it as you shall privately determine,
Either for her stay or going: the affair cries haste,
290   And speed must answer't: you must hence tonight.

DESD: Tonight, my lord?

DUKE: This night.

46

DESD: *I loved and married the Moor so I could live with him, as the world sees by the deliberate way I have upset my life. My heart was won even by the warlike qualities of my lord. In my mind's eye, I see Othello with his honors and valiant side, and to him I dedicated my soul and fortune. If he goes to war, and I am left behind, the very reason that I married him will be taken away from me. Let me go with him.*

OTHELLO: *Let her decide. Believe me, I am not saying this because this is what I want or out of lust, but to oblige her wishes. And, by heaven, do not think that I will neglect your serious and great business because she is with me. No, when the time comes that love slows my mind and affects my work, let housewives turn my helmet into a cooking pot and let everyone point out my shortcomings and belittle me.*

DUKE: *It is your private business, so you decide. Either she stays or goes, but the decision must be made quickly. You must leave tonight.*

DESD: [Surprised] *Tonight, my lord?*

DUKE: *This night.*

OTHELLO: With all my heart.

DUKE: At nine i' the morning here we'll meet again.
295   Othello, leave some officer behind,
And he shall our commission bring to you;
With such things else of quality and respect
As doth import you.

OTHELLO: So please your Grace, my ancient;
300   A man he is of honesty and trust.
To his conveyance I assign my wife,
With what else needful your good Grace shall think
To be sent after me.

DUKE: Let it be so.
305   Good night to everyone.
[To Brabantio] And, noble signior,
If virtue no delighted beauty lack,
Your son-in-law is far more fair than black.

FIRST SENATOR: Adieu, brave Moor, use Desdemona well.

310 BRAB: Look to her, Moor, if thou hast eyes to see;
She has deceived her father, and may thee.
[Exeunt Duke, Senators, and Officers.]

OTHELLO: My life upon her faith! Honest Iago,
My Desdemona must I leave to thee:
I prithee, let thy wife attend on her;
315   And bring them after in the best advantage.
Come, Desdemona, I have but an hour
Of love, of worldly matters and direction,
To spend with thee: We must obey the time.
[Exeunt Othello and Desdemona.]

ROD: Iago!

48

OTHELLO: [To Desdemona] *With all my heart.*

DUKE: *At nine in the morning, we will meet again. Othello, leave an officer here to handle your affairs, and we will give him the respect that we give you.*

OTHELLO: *If it pleases your Grace, my aid, Iago, is honest and trustworthy. To him I will assign the responsibility of bringing my wife and whatever else you may think I need.*

DUKE: *Let it be so. Good night, everyone.* [To Brabantio] *And noble sir, if virtue did not lack beauty, your son-in-law would be more fair than black.*

FIRST SENATOR: *Good-bye, brave Moor; take good care of Desdemona.*

BRAB: *Keep an eye on her, Moor, if you have eyes. She deceived her father and may deceive you.*

[Exit Duke of Venice, Senators, and Officers]

OTHELLO: *I'll bet my life upon her faithfulness! Honest Iago, I must leave my Desdemona with you. I beg you, let your wife wait on her and bring them when a good opportunity opens. Come Desdemona, I have only one hour of love and worldly matters to spend with you. We must obey the time.*

[Exit Othello and Desdemona]

ROD: *Iago!*

320 Iago: What say'st thou, noble heart?

Rod: What will I do, thinkest thou?

Iago: Why, go to bed and sleep.

Rod: I will incontinently drown myself.

Iago: If thou dost, I shall never love thee after.
325   Why, thou silly gentleman!

Rod: It is silliness to live when to live is torment, and then have we a prescription to die when death is our physician.

Iago: O villainous! I have looked upon the world for four times seven years, and since I could distinguish betwixt a benefit and an injury,
330   I never found man that knew how to love himself. Ere I would say I would drown myself for the love of a guinea hen, I would change my humanity with a baboon.

Rod: What should I do? I confess it is my shame to be so fond, but it is not in my virtue to amend it.

335 Iago: Virtue? a fig! 'Tis in ourselves that we are thus or thus. Our bodies are gardens, to the which our wills are gardeners; so that if we will plant nettles or sow lettuce, set hyssop and weed up thyme, supply it with one gender of herbs or distract it with many, either to have it sterile with idleness or manured with industry, why, the
340   power and corrigible authority of this lies in our wills. If the balance of our lives had not one scale of reason to poise another of sensuality, the blood and baseness of our natures would conduct us to most preposterous conclusions. But we have reason to cool our raging motions, our carnal stings, our unbitted lusts.

345 Rod: It cannot be.

Iago: It is merely a lust of the blood and a permission of the will.

50

IAGO: *What do you say, my good man?*

ROD: *What do you think I should do?*

IAGO: *Why, go to bed and sleep.*

ROD: *I will immediately drown myself.*

IAGO: *If you do, I will not be your friend, you foolish gentleman!*

ROD: *It is foolishness to live when living is torment, for when death is our doctor, we have a prescription to die.*

IAGO: *That is ridiculous! I have observed life for twenty-eight years, and ever since I have been able to tell the difference between a benefit and an injury, I never found a man who knew how to love himself. I would change places with a baboon before I would drown myself for the love of a female bird.*

ROD: *What should I do? I confess, it is shameful to be so much in love, but it is not my nature to change how I feel.*

IAGO: *Nature? Nature is worth nothing! It is we who decide if we are this or that. Our bodies are our gardens, and our wills are the gardeners. So if nettles or lettuce prick you, then you plant hyssop and pull up thyme: you plant other varieties, or you leave them to die or work around them. The power and authority to do all things is in our will. If we didn't have reason to balance our lust, our blood, and animal-like nature would make us do the most ridiculous things. But we have reason and thought to cool our raging emotions, our carnal thoughts, and our lustful urgings. I understand that this thing you call love is a mere offshoot of lust.*

ROD: *It cannot be.*

IAGO: *It is merely a lust of the body in which you are indulging through the per-*

Come, be a man! Drown thyself? Drown cats and blind puppies. I have professed me thy friend, and I confess me knit to thy deserving with cables of perdurable toughness; I could never better stead

350 thee than now. Put money in thy purse; follow thou the wars; defeat thy favor with an usurped beard. I say, put money in thy purse. It cannot be that Desdemona should long continue her love to the Moor—put money in thy purse—nor he his to her. It was a violent commencement, and thou shalt see an answerable seques-

355 tration; put but money in thy purse. These Moors are changeable in their wills:—fill thy purse with money. The food that to him now is as luscious as locusts, shall be to him shortly as acerb as the coloquintida. She must change for youth; when she is sated with his body, she will find the error of her choice. She must have change,

360 she must; therefore put money in thy purse. If thou wilt needs damn thyself, do it a more delicate way than drowning. Make all the money thou canst. If sanctimony and a frail vow betwixt an erring barbarian and a supersubtle Venetian be not too hard for my wits and all the tribe of hell, thou shalt enjoy her; therefore make

365 money. A pox of drowning thyself! It is clean out of the way. Seek thou rather to be hanged in compassing thy joy than to be drowned and go without her.

ROD: Wilt thou be fast to my hopes, if I depend on the issue?

IAGO: Thou art sure of me; go, make money. I have told thee often, and

370 I retell thee again and again, I hate the Moor. My cause is hearted; thine hath no less reason. Let us be conjunctive in our revenge against him. If thou canst cuckold him, thou dost thyself a pleasure, me a sport. There are many events in the womb of time which will be delivered. Traverse, go, provide thy money. We will have

375 more of this tomorrow. Adieu.

ROD: Where shall we meet i' the morning?

IAGO: At my lodging.

ROD: I'll be with thee betimes.

mission of your will. Come now, be a man! Drown yourself? We drown cats and blind puppies. I have told you that you are my friend, and now I am able to help you. Put some money in your pocket and follow the course of the wars, and stay sharp. I say, put some money in your pocket. It cannot be that Desdemona will be in love with Othello for long.—Put money in your pocket. Othello's love for her will not last. It was a rough beginning, and you will see it end the same way. Put money on that. These Moors change their minds often.—On that, fill your pocket with money. The food that he now finds tasty will soon be bitter as a cactus. She is young and will change her mind. When she is done with his body, she will see the mistake that she made. She must have variety; therefore, put money in your purse. If you must damn your soul, do it in a better way than killing yourself. Make all the money you can. A holy marriage vow between a barbarian and Venetian female will not be hard for my intelligence to find a way around. You will enjoy that woman. A curse on drowning yourself. Instead, seek to be hanged for indulging your joy with her, rather than to be drowned and go without her.

ROD: If I depend on you, are you sure you will work on my behalf?

IAGO: You can be sure of me: Go, make money. I have told you often, and I will say it again and again, I hate the Moor. I am happy about the way things are working out. You have no reason not to feel the same way. We are joined in our revenge against him. If you can win his wife, you will make yourself happier, and it will amuse me to see it. There are many events in the womb of time yet to be born. Get going! Get your money. We will speak more of this tomorrow. Goodnight.

ROD: Where will we meet in the morning?

IAGO: At my lodging.

ROD: I will be thinking about this in the meantime.

IAGO: Go to, farewell. Do you hear, Roderigo?

380 ROD: What say you?

IAGO: No more of drowning, do you hear?

ROD: I am changed; I'll go sell all my land.   [*Exit.*]

IAGO: Thus do I ever make my fool my purse;
For I mine own gain'd knowledge should profane,
385 If I would time expend with such a snipe
But for my sport and profit. I hate the Moor;
And it is thought abroad that 'twixt my sheets
He has done my office. I know not if't be true;
But I for mere suspicion in that kind
390 Will do as if for surety. He holds me well;
The better shall my purpose work on him.
Cassio's a proper man. Let me see now:
To get his place, and to plume up my will
In double knavery—How, how? —Let's see—
395 After some time, to abuse Othello's ear
That he is too familiar with his wife.
He hath a person and a smooth dispose
To be suspected; framed to make women false.
The Moor is of a free and open nature,
400 That thinks men honest that but seem to be so;
And will as tenderly be led by the nose
As asses are.
I have't. It is engender'd. Hell and night
Must bring this monstrous birth to the world's light.

                                        [*Exit.*]

❧

IAGO: Get going; farewell. Do you understand me, Roderigo?

ROD: What do you mean?

IAGO: No more talk of drowning; do you understand?

ROD: I have changed my mind about that. I'll go sell all my land.   [Exit]

IAGO: This is how I make my fool the source of money. Otherwise, spending time with such an idiot would be a shameful waste. I deal with him only for my entertainment and profit. I hate the Moor. Some people think that he has slept with my wife. I don't know if that is true, but for me, mere suspicion is equal to proof. Othello thinks highly of me. That is better for my plan to work on him. Cassio's a good man. Let me see now: How do I get his place and expand my plan into a double trickery—How, how? Let's see—At some point, I will deceive Othello by telling him that Cassio is too close to his wife. Cassio is just the kind of person with the smooth manners that might be suspected, just the type to make women cheat. The Moor has a free and generous nature. He thinks men are honest who only appear to be honest. Yes, he will be easily led by the nose like a mule. I have it. The plan is coming together. Hell and this night will see this monstrous plan born into the world's light.

[Exit]

ACT II

SCENE 1
A seaport in Cyprus.
An open place near the quay.

[Enter Montano and two Gentlemen.]

MONTANO: What from the cape can you discern at sea?

FIRST GENTLEMAN: Nothing at all. It is a highwrought flood;
I cannot, 'twixt the heaven and the main,
Descry a sail.

5   MONTANO: Methinks the wind hath spoke aloud at land;
A fuller blast ne'er shook our battlements:
If it hath ruffian'd so upon the sea,
What ribs of oak, when mountains melt on them,
Can hold the mortise? What shall we hear of this?

10   SECOND GENTLEMAN: A segregation of the Turkish fleet:
For do but stand upon the foaming shore,
The chidden billow seems to pelt the clouds;
The windshaked surge, with high and monstrous mane,
Seems to cast water on the burning bear,
15   And quench the guards of the everfixed pole:
I never did like molestation view
On the enchafed flood.

MONTANO: If that the Turkish fleet
Be not enshelter'd and embay'd, they are drown'd;
20   It is impossible to bear it out.

ACT II

SCENE 1
A Seaport in Cyprus.
An open place near the dock.

[Enter Montano and two Gentlemen]

MONTANO: *What can you tell about the sea from your view at the cape?*

FIRST GENTLEMAN: *Nothing at all. The waves are high and rough. I cannot spot a sail anywhere between heaven and the sea.*

MONTANO: *I think the wind said a lot to us when we were on land. A stronger blast of wind has never shaken our battlements. The wind has roughed up the sea so much, I wonder if ribbed ships can hold together when these mountains of waves crash on them? What have we heard about the ships?*

SECOND GENTLEMAN: *The Turkish fleet has broken up. Even though you stand only upon the foaming shore, you can see the waves of the water punished by the wind. The huge waves seemed to throw water so high that it hit the constellation Ursa Minor and the stars around the North Star. I never enjoy disturbing sights on the upset sea.*

MONTANO: *If the Turkish fleet is not sheltered in a safe bay, they are drowned. It is impossible they rode it out.*

[Enter a third Gentleman.]

THIRD GENTLEMAN: News, lads! Our wars are done.
      The desperate tempest hath so bang'd the Turks,
      That their designment halts: a noble ship of Venice
      Hath seen a grievous wreck and sufferance
25   On most part of their fleet.

MONTANO: How? Is this true?

THIRD GENTLEMAN: The ship is here put in;
      A Veronesa, Michael Cassio,
      Lieutenant to the warlike Moor, Othello,
30   Is come on shore; the Moor himself at sea,
      And is in full commission here for Cyprus.

MONTANO: I am glad on't; 'tis a worthy governor.

THIRD GENTLEMAN: But this same Cassio, though he speak of comfort
      Touching the Turkish loss, yet he looks sadly
35   And prays the Moor be safe; for they were parted
      With foul and violent tempest.

MONTANO: Pray heavens he be;
      For I have served him, and the man commands
      Like a full soldier. Let's to the seaside, ho!
40   As well to see the vessel that's come in
      As to throw out our eyes for brave Othello,
      Even till we make the main and the aerial blue
      An indistinct regard.

THIRD GENTLEMAN: Come, let's do so;
45   For every minute is expectancy
      Of more arrivance.

[Enter Cassio.]

58

[Enter a third Gentleman]

THIRD GENTLEMAN: *News, lads! Our wars are over. The desperate storm has so damaged the Turks that their attack plan is stopped. A noble ship of Venice has seen most of their fleet suffer a tremendous wreck.*

MONTANO: *How! Is this true?*

THIRD GENTLEMAN: *A ship has arrived. A man from Verona, Michael Cassio, Lieutenant to the mighty Moor, Othello, has come on shore. The Moor him-self is still at sea and sails at top speed to Cyprus.*

MONTANO: *I am glad about that. Othello is a worthy governor.*

THIRD GENTLEMAN: *But Cassio, even though what he says about the Turkish fleet is good news, looks sad, and he prays for the Moor's safety. They were separated by the violent storm.*

MONTANO: *Pray to the heavens for Othello's safety. I have served him, and the man commands like a perfect soldier. Let's go to the seawall. We will check the vessels that come in and keep an eye out for brave Othello. We'll do this for as long as we can tell the difference between the sea and the sky.*

THIRD GENTLEMAN: *Come, let's go; more ships arrive every minute.*

[Enter Cassio]

CASSIO: Thanks, you the valiant of this warlike isle,
    That so approve the Moor! O, let the heavens
    Give him defense against the elements,
50   For I have lost him on a dangerous sea.

MONTANO: Is he well shipp'd?

CASSIO: His bark is stoutly timber'd, and his pilot
    Of very expert and approved allowance;
    Therefore my hopes, not surfeited to death,
55   Stand in bold cure.
             [A cry within, "A sail, a sail, a sail!."]

[Enter a fourth Gentleman.]

CASSIO: What noise?

FOURTH GENTLEMAN: The town is empty; on the brow o' the sea
    Stand ranks of people, and they cry, "A sail!"

CASSIO: My hopes do shape him for the governor. *[Guns heard.]*

60   SECOND GENTLEMAN: They do discharge their shot of courtesy:
    Our friends at least.

CASSIO: I pray you, sir, go forth,
    And give us truth who 'tis that is arrived.

THIRD GENTLEMAN: I shall.   *[Exit.]*

MONTANO: But, good lieutenant, is your general wived?

65   CASSIO: Most fortunately: he hath achieved a maid
    That paragons description and wild fame;
    One that excels the quirks of blazoning pens,
    And in the essential vesture of creation
    Does tire the ingener.

CASSIO: *Thanks to you, the valiant people of this warlike isle, who so appreciate the Moor! Oh, let the heavens guard him against the elements, for I have lost him on the dangerous sea.*

MONTANO: *Is his ship a sturdy one?*

CASSIO: *His boat has thick timbers, and his pilot is an expert and very experienced. Therefore, my hopes, although not absolutely confident, make me feel secure.*

[A cry within 'A sail, a sail, a sail!']

[Enter a fourth Gentleman]

CASSIO: *What was that noise?*

FOURTH GENTLEMAN: *The town is empty. Everyone is at the edge of the sea, and they are yelling, "A sail!"*

CASSIO: *I hope I will see the governor, Othello, standing there.* [Guns heard]

SECOND GENTLEMEN: *They fired their shot of courtesy. At least we know they are our friends.*

CASSIO: *I beg you, sir, go forward and tell us truthfully who has arrived.*

THIRD GENTLEMAN: *I shall.*   [Exit]

MONTANO: *But, good lieutenant, is your general married?*

CASSIO: *In that he is a very lucky man. He has won a maiden whose beauty outdoes description and wild fame—a beauty that goes beyond the ability of pens to record and tires the creator to depict.*

[Reenter second Gentleman.]
70   How now! who has put in?

SECOND GENTLEMAN: 'Tis one Iago, ancient to the general.

CASSIO: He has had most favorable and happy speed:
Tempests themselves, high seas, and howling winds,
The gutter'd rocks, and congregated sands,
75   Traitors ensteep'd to clog the guiltless keel,
As having sense of beauty, do omit
Their mortal natures, letting go safely by
The divine Desdemona.

MONTANO: What is she?

80   CASSIO: She that I spake of, our great captain's captain,
Left in the conduct of the bold Iago;
Whose footing here anticipates our thoughts
A se'nnight's speed. Great Jove, Othello guard,
And swell his sail with thine own powerful breath,
85   That he may bless this bay with his tall ship,
Make love's quick pants in Desdemona's arms,
Give renew'd fire to our extincted spirits,
And bring all Cyprus comfort.

[Enter Desdemona, Emilia Iago, Roderigo, and Attendants]
O, behold,
90   The riches of the ship is come on shore!
Ye men of Cyprus, let her have your knees.
Hail to thee, lady! And the grace of heaven,
Before, behind thee, and on every hand,
Enwheel thee round!

95   DESD: I thank you, valiant Cassio.
What tidings can you tell me of my lord?

CASSIO: He is not yet arrived; nor know I aught
But that he's well and will be shortly here.

[Reenter second Gentleman]
How are things now! Who has arrived in the harbor?

SECOND GENTLEMAN: It is Iago, an aide to the general.

CASSIO: He has made very good time. The storms themselves, the high seas, and howling winds, the guttered rocks and beaches–all dangers attempting to wreck ships–have gone against their nature, sensed her beauty, and let the divine Desdemona go safely by.

MONTANO: Who is she?

CASSIO: The woman I spoke of is our great captain's captain, who was left in the safe care of the bold Iago. She is landing here seven days before we anticipated her. Great Jove, guard Othello and fill his sails with your own powerful breath so that he may bless this bay with his tall ship. May he breathe easy in Desdemona's arms, give renewed fire to our low spirits, and bring all Cyprus comfort!

[Enter Desdemona, Emilia, Iago, Roderigo, and Attendants]
Oh, behold, the riches of the ship have come on shore! You men of Cyprus, kneel in front of her. Hail to you, lady! May the grace of heaven surround you.

DESD: I thank you, valiant Cassio. What information can you tell me about Othello?

CASSIO: He has not yet arrived, nor do I know when he will arrive, or even if he is safe.

DESD: O, but I fear—How lost you company?

100 CASSIO: The great contention of the sea and skies
    Parted our fellowship—But, hark! a sail.
            [A cry within, "A sail, a sail!" Guns heard.]

SECOND GENTLEMAN: They give their greeting to the citadel:
    This likewise is a friend.

CASSIO: See for the news.   *[Exit Gentleman.]*
105   Good ancient, you are welcome. *[To Emilia.]* Welcome, mistress.
    Let it not gall your patience, good Iago,
    That I extend my manners; 'tis my breeding
    That gives me this bold show of courtesy.   *[Kisses her.]*

IAGO: Sir, would she give you so much of her lips
110   As of her tongue she oft bestows on me,
    You'd have enough.

DESD: Alas, she has no speech.

IAGO: In faith, too much;
    I find it still when I have list to sleep:
115   Marry, before your ladyship, I grant
    She puts her tongue a little in her heart
    And chides with thinking.

EMILIA: You have little cause to say so.

IAGO: Come on, come on. You are pictures out of doors,
120   Bells in your parlors, wildcats in your kitchens,
    Saints in your injuries, devils being offended,
    Players in your housewifery, and housewives in your beds.

DESD: O, fie upon thee, slanderer!

IAGO: Nay, it is true, or else I am a Turk:
125   You rise to play, and go to bed to work.

DESD: Oh, I'm afraid—How did you get separated?

CASSIO: The great struggle between the sea and skies parted us—But, look! A sail. [Shouts of, "A sail, a sail!" Guns are heard]

SECOND GENTLEMAN: They are signaling the fortress. This is also a friend.

CASSIO: Go see who it is.   [Exit Gentleman]
[To Iago] My good ensign, you are welcome in Cypress. [To Emilia] Welcome, good lady. [To Iago] Do not be annoyed, good Iago, that I extend my manners to your wife. I was raised to make this type of show of courtesy. [Kissing her]

IAGO: Sir, if she gave you as much of her lips as she gives her voice to me, you'd soon have enough.

DESD: It is too bad she does not speak up for herself.

IAGO: Honestly, she speaks up too much; it happens most often when I want to sleep. Although, by your ladyship, I admit that her words are somewhat kind, and her scolds are in her thoughts.

EMILIA: You have no reason to say that.

IAGO: Come on, come on; you women are pretty painted pictures out-of-doors, decorations in your parlors, wild cats in your kitchens, saints when nursing injuries, and devils when offended. You all are actors when performing your housewife duties and loose women in your beds.

DESD: Oh, to hell with you, slanderer!

IAGO: No, it is true, or else I am a Turk. You get up to play and go to bed to work.

EMILIA: You shall not write my praise.

IAGO: No, let me not.

DESD: What wouldst thou write of me, if thou shouldst praise me?

IAGO: O gentle lady, do not put me to't;
130   For I am nothing if not critical.

DESD: Come on, assay—There's one gone to the harbor?

IAGO: Ay, madam.

DESD: I am not merry, but I do beguile
     The thing I am by seeming otherwise.
135   Come, how wouldst thou praise me?

IAGO: I am about it; but indeed my invention
     Comes from my pate as birdlime does from frieze;
     It plucks out brains and all. But my Muse labors,
     And thus she is deliver'd.
140   If she be fair and wise, fairness and wit,
     The one's for use, the other useth it.

DESD: Well praised! How if she be black and witty?

IAGO: If she be black, and thereto have a wit,
     She'll find a white that shall her blackness fit.

145 DESD: Worse and worse.

EMILIA: How if fair and foolish?

IAGO: She never yet was foolish that was fair;
     For even her folly help'd her to an heir.

EMILIA: *You will not make an estimate of me.*

IAGO: *No, I will not.*

DESD: *What would you write about me, if you were to praise me?*

IAGO: *Oh, gentle lady, do not ask me to do that because I am nothing, if not critical.*

DESD: *Come on, let's hear it.* [Suddenly] *Has someone gone to the harbor to watch for Othello?*

IAGO: *Yes, madam.*

DESD: [Aside] *I am not happy, but I am able to disguise what I am by seeming different. Come on, how would you praise me?*

IAGO: *I'll give it a try; but the things I think up come from my head, as sticky as birdlime that plucks out brains and everything else. Let's see—my inspiration labors and delivers this. If she is fair and wise; she shows wisdom by using her wit well.*

DESD: *Well praised! What if she were black and witty?*

IAGO: *If she is black and also has a wit, she'll find a white that will fit her blackness.*

DESD: *It gets worse and worse.*

EMILIA: *What if she is fair and foolish?*

IAGO: *A pretty girl is never foolish, for even in her folly she will conceive an heir.*

Desd: These are old fond paradoxes to make fools laugh i' the ale-
150 house. What miserable praise hast thou for her that's foul and foolish?

Iago: There's none so foul and foolish thereunto,
   But does foul pranks which fair and wise ones do.

Desd: O heavy ignorance! Thou praisest the worst best. But what
155 praise couldst thou bestow on a deserving woman indeed, one that
in the authority of her merit did justly put on the vouch of very
malice itself?

Iago: She that was ever fair and never proud,
   Had tongue at will and yet was never loud,
160 Never lack'd gold and yet went never gay,
   Fled from her wish and yet said, "Now I may";
   She that, being anger'd, her revenge being nigh,
   Bade her wrong stay and her displeasure fly;
   She that in wisdom never was so frail
165 To change the cod's head for the salmon's tail;
   She that could think and ne'er disclose her mind,
   See suitors following and not look behind;
   She was a wight, if ever such wight were—

Desd: To do what?

170 Iago: To suckle fools and chronicle small beer.

Desd: O most lame and impotent conclusion! Do not learn of him,
   Emilia, though he be thy husband. How say you, Cassio? Is he not
a most profane and liberal counselor?

Cassio: He speaks home, madam. You may relish him more in the sol-
175 dier than in the scholar.

Iago: [Aside.] He takes her by the palm; ay, well said, whisper. With as
little a web as this will I ensnare as great a fly as Cassio. Ay, smile

68

DESD: *These are old jokes intended to make fools laugh in the alehouse. What miserable praise do you have for a woman that is foul and foolish?*

IAGO: *No woman is very foul and foolish, unless she does the foul pranks that fair and wise women do.*

DESD: *Oh, this is ignorance! You describe the worst best. But what praise could you give a deserving woman who, using the power of her good qualities, has safely guarded herself against trouble?*

IAGO: *She who was always pretty, never proud; she who could have said much but never did; she who always had money but never showed it off; she who ran away from what her family wished, but yet could say, "Now I may;" she who did not take revenge when angry, could forgive wrongs, and forget her displeasure; she who was smart enough never to make foolish decisions; she that could think quite well but never revealed what she was thinking; she who could see suitors following and not look behind. She was a person, if ever such a person were—*

DESD: *To do what?*

IAGO: *To nurse babies and keep track of small household expenses.*

DESD: *Oh, this is a most lame and weak conclusion! Do not listen to him, Emilia, even though he is your husband. What do you say, Cassio? Isn't he a most blasphemous and vulgar counselor?*

CASSIO: *His speech is plain, madam. You may appreciate him more as a soldier than a scholar.*

IAGO: *[Aside] He takes her by the hand. Yes, well done, whisper to her. With this small web of truth I will ensnare a fly as big as Cassio. Yes, smile at her;*

69

180 upon her, do; I will gyve thee in thine own courtship. You say true; 'tis so, indeed. If such tricks as these strip you out of your lieu-tenantry, it had been better you had not kissed your three fingers so oft, which now again you are most apt to play the sir in. Very good. Well kissed! an excellent courtesy! 'tis so, indeed. Yet again your fingers to your lips? Would they were clysterpipes for your sake! *[Trumpet within.]* The Moor! I know his trumpet.

185 CASSIO: 'Tis truly so.

DESD: Let's meet him and receive him.

CASSIO: Lo, where he comes!

[Enter Othello and Attendants.]

OTHELLO: O my fair warrior!

DESD: My dear Othello!

190 OTHELLO: It gives me wonder great as my content
To see you here before me. O my soul's joy!
If after every tempest come such calms,
May the winds blow till they have waken'd death!
And let the laboring bark climb hills of seas
195 Olympus high, and duck again as low
As hell's from heaven! If it were now to die,
Twere now to be most happy; for I fear
My soul hath her content so absolute
That not another comfort like to this
200 Succeeds in unknown fate.

DESD: The heavens forbid
But that our loves and comforts should increase,
Even as our days do grow!

OTHELLO: Amen to that, sweet powers!

I will shackle you in your own courtship. You say it is your upbringing to treat women so, all right, Cassio, if these tricks take away your position of lieutenant, you will have wished that you had not kissed the ladies' fingers so often. Very good, well kissed! An excellent courtesy! Yes, it is indeed–and again her fingers to your lips? When this is over, you will wish that they were enema tubes! [Trumpet within] *The Moor! I know his trumpet.*

CASSIO: *It is true.*

DESD: *Let's meet him and welcome him.*

CASSIO: *There, he is coming up!*

[Enter Othello and Attendants]

OTHELLO: *Oh, my fair warrior!*

DESD: *My dear Othello!*

OTHELLO: *I am as amazed as I am happy to see you here in front of me. Oh, my soul's joy! If this calm came after every storm, then let the winds blow till they have awakened death! And let the laboring ship climb waves as high as Mount Olympus and then fall again as low as hell is from heaven! If I were to die now, I would die a happy man because I am afraid that my soul is so absolutely content that no other comfort like this could come to me in the future.*

DESD: *The heavens forbid everything except that our love and happiness should increase, as our days grow!*

OTHELLO: *Amen to that, sweet powers! I cannot say how happy I am. It stops*

205   I cannot speak enough of this content;
        It stops me here; it is too much of joy:
        And this, and this, the greatest discords be
        [Kisses her.] That e'er our hearts shall make!

        IAGO: *[Aside.]* O, you are well tuned now!
210   But I'll set down the pegs that make this music,
        As honest as I am.

        OTHELLO: Come, let us to the castle.
        News, friends: our wars are done, the Turks are drown'd.
        Honey, you shall be well desired in Cyprus;
215   I have found great love amongst them. O my sweet,
        I prattle out of fashion, and I dote
        In mine own comforts. I prithee, good Iago,
        Go to the bay and disembark my coffers:
        Bring thou the master to the citadel;
220   He is a good one, and his worthiness
        Does challenge much respect. Come, Desdemona,
        Once more well met at Cyprus. *[Exeunt all but Iago and Roderigo.]*

        IAGO: Do thou meet me presently at the harbor. Come hither. If thou
        be'st valiant—as they say base men being in love have then a nobil-
225   ity in their natures more than is native to them—list me. The lieu-
        tenant tonight watches on the court of guard. First, I must tell thee
        this: Desdemona is directly in love with him.

        ROD: With him? Why, 'tis not possible.

        IAGO: Lay thy finger thus, and let thy soul be instructed. Mark me with
230   what violence she first loved the Moor, but for bragging and telling
        her fantastical lies. And will she love him still for prating? Let not
        thy discreet heart think it. Her eye must be fed; and what delight
        shall she have to look on the devil? When the blood is made dull
        with the act of sport, there should be, again to inflame it and to give
235   satiety a fresh appetite, loveliness in favor, sympathy in years, man-
        ners, and beauties; all which the Moor is defective in. Now, for

me here; it is too much joy. May this be the greatest conflict that we ever have! [Kissing her]

IAGO: [Aside] *Oh, you are well tuned now! But I will unscrew the pegs that make this music, as honest as I am.*

OTHELLO: *Come, let us go to the castle. Good news, my friends; our wars are done, and the Turks have drowned. How is my friend on this land?* [To Desdemona] *Honey, you will be well liked in Cyprus; I have found them to be a very generous people. Oh, my sweet, I am chattering impolitely, and I am indulging my own happiness. I beg you, good Iago, go to the bay and get my baggage. Bring my things and the captain of the ship to the castle. He is a good captain, and his excellent seamanship demands a great deal of respect. Come, Desdemona; once again, it is good to be in Cyprus.* [Exit all but Iago and Roderigo]

IAGO: *Meet me at the harbor. Roderigo, Come here. If you are a valiant man— and they say that common men when they are in love have more nobility in their natures than what is normal for them—listen to me. The lieutenant tonight has the responsibility of guarding the court—first, I have to tell you this—Desdemona is absolutely in love with him.*

ROD: *With him! Why, it is not possible.*

IAGO: [Putting a finger to his lips] *Lay your finger here, and listen to me. Remember how strongly she first loved the Moor because of his bragging and telling her fantastic lies. Do you think she will still love him for chattering? Don't let your heart shy away from thinking about it. She must have something attractive to look at. How delightful can it be for her to look at the devil? When her desires have been calmed after love, she will need to excite it and give herself a fresh appetite. She needs someone who is handsome in appearance, is closer to her own age, and has polite manners; all of* want of these required conveniences, her delicate tenderness will find itself abused, begin to heave the gorge, disrelish and abhor the Moor; very nature will instruct her in it and compel her to some

240   second choice. Now sir, this granted—as it is a most pregnant and unforced position—who stands so eminently in the degree of this fortune as Cassio does? A knave very voluble; no further conscionable than in putting on the mere form of civil and humane seeming, for the better compassing of his salt and most hidden

245   loose affection? Why, none; why, none; a slipper and subtle knave, a finder out of occasions; that has an eye can stamp and counterfeit advantages, though true advantage never present itself: a devilish knave! Besides, the knave is handsome, young, and hath all those requisites in him that folly and green minds look after; a

250   pestilent complete knave; and the woman hath found him already.

ROD: I cannot believe that in her; she's full of most blest condition.

IAGO: Blest fig'send! The wine she drinks is made of grapes. If she had been blest, she would never have loved the Moor. Blest pudding! Didst thou not see her paddle with the palm of his hand? Didst not

255   mark that?

ROD: Yes, that I did; but that was but courtesy.

IAGO: Lechery, by this hand; an index and obscure prologue to the history of lust and foul thoughts. They met so near with their lips that their breaths embraced together. Villainous thoughts, Roderigo!

260   When these mutualities so marshal the way, hard at hand comes the master and main exercise, the incorporate conclusion. Pish! But, sir, be you ruled by me. I have brought you from Venice. Watch you tonight; for the command, I'll lay't upon you. Cassio knows you not. I'll not be far from you. Do you find some occasion

265   to anger Cassio, either by speaking too loud, or tainting his discipline, or from what other course you please, which the time shall more favorably minister.

ROD: Well.

which the Moor lacks. Now, because she will miss these qualities, her delicate love will be feel cheated, she will get sick, begin to vomit, and hate the Moor. Her innate character will instruct her and force her to take some second choice. Now, sir, given this situation—since it is an obvious and likely position—who has a better opportunity here than Cassio? What other scoundrel would be in a better position to pretend to be well mannered and polite in order to fulfill his own obscene desires? No one, no one! He is a slippery and sneaky scoundrel, an opportunist, with the ability to fake and create phony advantages, even when true advantage never presents itself. He's a devilish rascal. Besides, the villain is handsome, young, and has all those qualities that fools and young minds look for. He is a sickening and absolute rogue, and Desdemona has found him already.

ROD: I cannot believe that she act that way. She is full of holy qualities.

IAGO: "Holy" she is not! She is not a saint or goddess. If she were so good, she would never have fallen in love with the Moor. "Holy"; Nonsense! Didn't you see her play with the palm of his hand? Didn't you notice that?

ROD: Yes, I did; but that was only good manners.

IAGO: It was lust, and in so doing she sent a signal and subtle preview to match his history of lust and foul thoughts. They came so close with their lips that their breaths embraced. Terrible thoughts, Roderigo! With their lustful exchanges leading the way toward the main exercise, surely the two bodies will inevitably come together. Pish! But, sir, listen to me: I have brought you from Venice. Watch tonight for when Cassio is on guard duty. I'll give you the plan. Cassio doesn't know you. [Roderigo makes a face]—Don't worry, I'll be close by you. Find some reason to make Cassio angry, either by speaking too loud, or taunting his discipline or however you please, based on what seems best for the time.

ROD: Good.

IAGO: Sir, he is rash and very sudden in choler, and haply may strike
270   at you. Provoke him, that he may; for even out of that will I cause
these of Cyprus to mutiny, whose qualification shall come into no
true taste again but by the displanting of Cassio. So shall you have
a shorter journey to your desires by the means I shall then have to
prefer them, and the impediment most profitably removed, without
275   the which there were no expectation of our prosperity.

ROD: I will do this, if I can bring it to any opportunity.

IAGO: I warrant thee. Meet me by and by at the citadel. I must fetch his
necessaries ashore. Farewell.

ROD: Adieu.   *[Exit.]*

280   IAGO: That Cassio loves her, I do well believe it;
       That she loves him, 'tis apt and of great credit:
       The Moor, howbeit that I endure him not,
       Is of a constant, loving, noble nature;
       And I dare think he'll prove to Desdemona
285   A most dear husband. Now, I do love her too,
       Not out of absolute lust, though peradventure
       I stand accountant for as great a sin,
       But partly led to diet my revenge,
       For that I do suspect the lusty Moor
290   Hath leap'd into my seat; the thought whereof
       Doth like a poisonous mineral gnaw my inwards,
       And nothing can or shall content my soul
       Till I am even'd with him, wife for wife;
       Or failing so, yet that I put the Moor
295   At least into a jealousy so strong
       That judgement cannot cure. Which thing to do,
       If this poor trash of Venice, whom I trash
       For his quick hunting, stand the putting on,
       I'll have our Michael Cassio on the hip,
300   Abuse him to the Moor in the rank garb:
       For I fear Cassio with my nightcap too;

IAGO: *Sir, Cassio is rash and has a quick temper, and he may hit you. Provoke him, so that he does. Even with that small action, I will get these soldiers to mutiny and force Othello to get rid of Cassio. So you will have a shorter journey to your Desdemona by having had the main obstacle easily removed. Without removing him, there is no reason to think that we will succeed.*

ROD: *I will do this, if I can find the opportunity.*

IAGO: *I believe this. Meet me later at the castle; I must bring his belongings ashore. Farewell.*

ROD: *Adieu.*   [Exit]

IAGO: *I do believe that Cassio loves her, and it is likely and believable that she loves him,. The Moor, even though I cannot stand him, has a constant, loving, noble nature, and I think he will prove to be a good husband to Desdemona. I love Desdemona, too. Not out of complete lust, but because I have committed as great a sin, I need to have revenge. I suspect the lusty Moor has leaped into my wife's bed; and the thought of that is eating away at my guts like a poison. Nothing will satisfy me except getting even with him, wife for wife. Or if I can't do that, then I want to put the Moor into a jealousy so strong that he loses his common sense. Which plan should be first? If this poor trash of Venice, Roderigo, whom I have on a leash, is able to make Cassio angry enough, I'll have Michael Cassio in my pocket. I will denounce him to the Moor in the worst possible way—for I fear Cassio has been in my bed, too. I'll make the Moor thank me, love me, and reward me for tricking him into appearing to be such an enormous ass and turning his peace and quiet to madness. It is all here, but still mixed up; trickery's true face is not clearly seen until it is used.*   [Exit]

Make the Moor thank me, love me, and reward me,
For making him egregiously an ass
And practicing upon his peace and quiet
305   Even to madness. 'Tis here, but yet confused:
Knavery's plain face is never seen till used.

[Exit.]

SCENE 2
A street.

[Enter a Herald with a proclamation; people following.]

HERALD: It is Othello's pleasure, our noble and valiant general, that
upon certain tidings now arrived, importing the mere perdition of
the Turkish fleet, every man put himself into triumph; some to
dance, some to make bonfires, each man to what sport and revels
5   his addiction leads him; for besides these beneficial news, it is the
celebration of his nuptial. So much was his pleasure should be proclaimed. All offices are open, and there is full liberty of feasting
from this present hour of five till the bell have told eleven. Heaven
bless the isle of Cyprus and our noble general Othello!

[Exeunt]

SCENE 3
A hall in the castle.

[Enter Othello, Desdemona, Cassio, and Attendants.]

OTHELLO: Good Michael, look you to the guard tonight:
Let's teach ourselves that honorable stop,
Not to outsport discretion.

CASSIO: Iago hath direction what to do;
5   But notwithstanding with my personal eye
Will I look to't.

SCENE 2
A street.

[Enter a Herald with a proclamation; People following]

HERALD: *It is our noble and valiant general, Othello's wish, that with the recent news of the destruction of the Turkish fleet, every man should begin to celebrate. Some may dance, some may make bonfires, but each man is to celebrate however he wants. For in addition to the good news about the Turks, this is a celebration of his marriage. Therefore, he has proclaimed a holiday: all offices are closed, and the public is free to feast from this present hour of five until the bells have chimed eleven o'clock. Heaven bless the island of Cyprus and our noble general Othello!*

[Exeunt]

SCENE 3
A hall in the castle.

[Enter Othello, Desdemona, Cassio, and Attendants]

OTHELLO: *Good Michael, you are in charge of the patrol tonight. Let your example demonstrate that honorable men know when to stop celebrating and not get carried away.*

CASSIO: *Iago has been told what to do. But, regardless of that, I will take care of things myself.*

OTHELLO: Iago is most honest.
Michael, good night. Tomorrow with your earliest
Let me have speech with you. Come, my dear love,
10   The purchase made, the fruits are to ensue;
That profit's yet to come 'tween me and you.
Good night.   *[Exeunt Othello, Desdemona, and Attendants.]*

[Enter Iago]

CASSIO: Welcome, Iago; we must to the watch.

IAGO: Not this hour, lieutenant; 'tis not yet ten o' the clock. Our gen-
15   eral cast us thus early for the love of his Desdemona; who let us not
therefore blame. He hath not yet made wanton the night with her,
and she is sport for Jove.

CASSIO: She's a most exquisite lady.

IAGO: And, I'll warrant her, full of game.

20   CASSIO: Indeed she's a most fresh and delicate creature.

IAGO: What an eye she has!
Methinks it sounds a parley to provocation.

CASSIO: An inviting eye; and yet methinks right modest.

IAGO: And when she speaks, is it not an alarum to love?

25   CASSIO: She is indeed perfection.

IAGO: Well, happiness to their sheets! Come, lieutenant, I have a stoup
of wine, and here without are a brace of Cyprus gallants that would
fain have a measure to the health of black Othello.

CASSIO: Not tonight, good Iago: I have very poor and unhappy brains
30   for drinking. I could well wish courtesy would invent some other
custom of entertainment.

OTHELLO: Iago is very honest. Michael, good night. Early tomorrow I need to have a meeting with you. [To Desdemona] Come, my dear love, the purchase has been made, so the fruits will follow. The benefit has not yet come between you and me. Good night.

[Exit Othello, Desdemona, and Attendants]

[Enter Iago]

CASSIO: Welcome, Iago; we must go on patrol.

IAGO: Not yet, lieutenant; it is not ten o'clock yet. Our general sent us out early because of his love for Desdemona; therefore, we should not blame him. He has not yet made love this night with her, and she is ready for romance.

CASSIO: She's a most exquisite lady.

IAGO: And, I'll bet she is full of spirit.

CASSIO: Indeed, she's a fresh and delicate creature.

IAGO: What an eye she has! I think it speaks of seduction.

CASSIO: She has an inviting eye, and yet I think she is modest.

IAGO: And when she speaks, doesn't it sound like a call to love?

CASSIO: She is indeed perfection.

IAGO: Well, happiness to their sheets! Come, lieutenant, I have a bottle of wine, and outside is a group of Cypriot gentlemen who would like to drink to Othello's health.

CASSIO: Not tonight, good Iago. I do not hold my alcohol well. I sincerely wish some custom other than drinking could be invented for entertainment.

IAGO: O, they are our friends! But one cup; I'll drink for you.

CASSIO: I have drunk but one cup tonight, and that was craftily quali-
fied too, and behold what innovation it makes here. I am unfortu-
35   nate in the infirmity, and dare not task my weakness with any more.

IAGO: What, man! 'Tis a night of revels, the gallants desire it.

CASSIO: Where are they?

IAGO: Here at the door; I pray you, call them in.

CASSIO: I'll do't, but it dislikes me.   [Exit.]

40   IAGO: If I can fasten but one cup upon him,
        With that which he hath drunk tonight already,
        He'll be as full of quarrel and offense
        As my young mistress' dog. Now my sick foolRoderigo,
        Whom love hath turn'd almost the wrong side out,
45   To Desdemona hath tonight caroused
        Potations pottledeep; and he's to watch:
        Three lads of Cyprus, noble swelling spirits,
        That hold their honors in a wary distance,
        The very elements of this warlike isle,
50   Have I tonight fluster'd with flowing cups,
        And they watch too. Now, 'mongst this flock of drunkards,
        Am I to put our Cassio in some action
        That may offend the isle. But here they come:
        If consequence do but approve my dream,
55   My boat sails freely, both with wind and stream.

[Reenter Cassio; with him Montano and Gentlemen; Servants following
with wine.]

CASSIO: 'Fore God, they have given me a rouse already.

IAGO: Oh, they are our friends; just one cup. I'll drink it for you.

CASSIO: I have already had one cup tonight, and I was tricked into drinking that. Look what changes it has made. I am unfortunate in my weakness, and do not dare risk drinking any more.

IAGO: What, man! It is a night of partying. It is what the visiting gentlemen desire.

CASSIO: Where are they?

IAGO: Here at the door. I beg you, call them in.

CASSIO: I'll do it, but I don't like this.   [Exit]

IAGO: If I can get even one cup in him, with what he has drunk tonight already, he'll be as ready to fight as my young mistress' dog. Now, my sick fool, Roderigo, whom love has turned inside out, has drunk many toasts to Desdemona, and he has with him three young men of Cyprus, who are in good spirits, and consider honor a very sensitive subject. I have made these elements of this warlike island drunk with flowing cups of wine. Now, among this flock of drunkards, I need to get Cassio to do something that will offend the people of this island. But here they come; if it works out the way I have planned, my boat sails easily, pushed by both the wind and the current.

[Reenter Cassio; with him Montano and Gentlemen; servants following with wine]

CASSIO: I swear before God, they have given me a drink already.

MONTANO: Good faith, a little one; not past a pint, as I am a soldier.

IAGO: Some wine, ho!

    [Sings.]   "And let me the canakin clink, clink;
60   And let me the canakin clink:
                      A soldier's a man;
                      O, man's life's but a span;
               Why then let a soldier drink."
    Some wine, boys!

65   CASSIO: 'Fore God, an excellent song.

IAGO: I learned it in England, where indeed they are most potent in potting. Your Dane, your German, and your swagbellied Hollander—Drink, ho!—are nothing to your English.

CASSIO: Is your Englishman so expert in his drinking?

70   IAGO: Why, he drinks you with facility your Dane dead drunk; he sweats not to overthrow your Almain; he gives your Hollander a vomit ere the next pottle can be filled.

CASSIO: To the health of our general!

MONTANO: I am for it, lieutenant, and I'll do you justice.

75   IAGO: O sweet England!

    [Sings.]   "King Stephen was a worthy peer,
                   His breeches cost him but a crown;
              He held them sixpence all too dear,
                 With that he call'd the tailor lown.
80   "He was a wight of high renown,
                 And thou art but of low degree:
      'Tis pride that pulls the country down;
        Then take thine auld cloak about thee."
    Some wine, ho!

MONTANO: *In good faith, drink a little one. Not larger than a pint, you have my word as a soldier.*

IAGO: *Some wine, ho!*
    [Sings]   *"And let me the cups clink, clink;*
                     And let me the cups clink
                     A soldier's a man;
                     A man's life's but a span;
                     Why, then, let a soldier drink."
    [Picking up the bottle and offering it around] *Some wine, boys!*

CASSIO: [Somewhat drunk] *Before God, an excellent song.*

IAGO: *I learned it in England, where, indeed, they are serious drinkers. Your Dane, your German, and your pot-bellied Dutchman—*[Raising a glass] *Drink, ho!—are nothing to your English.*

CASSIO: *Is your Englishman so expert in his drinking?*

IAGO: *Why, he easily outdrinks your dead drunk Dane; he does not break a sweat to out-drink a German; and he will make your Hollander vomit before the next bottle can be filled.*

CASSIO: *To the health of our general!* [He drinks]

MONTANO: *I am for it, lieutenant, and I'll match your toast.*

IAGO: *Oh, sweet England!*

[He sings]   *"King Stephen was a worthy peer,*
                     His pants cost him but a crown;
                He felt sixpence was all too dear,
                     With that he called the tailor down.
                He was a man of high renown,
                     And you are nothing but low degree:
             It's pride that pulls the country down;
             Then put your old cloak around you."
      Some wine, ho!

85 CASSIO: Why, this is a more exquisite song than the other.

IAGO: Will you hear't again?

CASSIO: No, for I hold him to be unworthy of his place that does those things. Well, God's above all, and there be souls must be saved, and there be souls must not be saved.

90 IAGO: It's true, good lieutenant.

CASSIO: For mine own part—no offense to the general, nor any man of quality—I hope to be saved.

IAGO: And so do I too, lieutenant.

CASSIO: Ay, but, by your leave, not before me; the lieutenant is to be
95   saved before the ancient. Let's have no more of this; let's to our affairs. God forgive us our sins! Gentlemen, let's look to our business. Do not think, gentlemen, I am drunk: this is my ancient, this is my right hand, and this is my left. I am not drunk now; I can stand well enough, and I speak well enough.

100 ALL: Excellent well.

CASSIO: Why, very well then; you must not think then that I am drunk.
                                                              [Exit.]

MONTANO: To the platform, masters; come, let's set the watch.

IAGO: You see this fellow that is gone before;
      He is a soldier fit to stand by Caesar
105   And give direction. And do but see his vice;
      'Tis to his virtue a just equinox,
      The one as long as the other. 'Tis pity of him.
      I fear the trust Othello puts him in
      On some odd time of his infirmity
110   Will shake this island.

CASSIO: *Why, this is a better song than the other.*

IAGO: *Do you want to hear it again?*

CASSIO: *No, because I do not have any respect for a man that drinks and sings like this. Well, God's above all, and there are souls which must be saved, and there are souls which must not be saved.*

IAGO: *It's true, good lieutenant.*

CASSIO: *For my own part,—no offense to the general, nor any man of quality,— I hope to be saved.*

IAGO: *And so do I, lieutenant.*

CASSIO: *Yes, but, by your permission, not before me; the lieutenant should be saved before the ensign. Let's have no more of this; let's attend to our affairs. God forgive our sins! Gentlemen, let's take care of our business. Do not think, gentlemen, that I am drunk. This is my ensign; this is my right hand, and this is my left. I am not drunk now; I can stand well enough, and speak well enough.*

ALL: *Excellent!*

CASSIO: *Why, very well then. You must not think that I am drunk.* [Exit]

MONTANO: *To the platform, friends; come, let's send out the patrol.*

IAGO: [To the others] *You see this fellow, Cassio, who has just left. He is a soldier fit to stand by Caesar and give orders; but do you see his defect? It is equal to his virtue, one is as long as the other. It is a pity. I am afraid that the trust Othello puts in Cassio, once when he is drunk, will cause trouble for this island.*

MONTANO: But is he often thus?

IAGO: 'Tis evermore the prologue to his sleep;
   He'll watch the horologe a double set,
   If drink rock not his cradle.

115 MONTANO: It were well
      The general were put in mind of it.
      Perhaps he sees it not, or his good nature
      Prizes the virtue that appears in Cassio
      And looks not on his evils: Is not this true?

[Enter Roderigo]

120 IAGO: *[Aside to him.]* How now, Roderigo!
      I pray you, after the lieutenant; go.   *[Exit Roderigo]*

MONTANO: And 'tis great pity that the noble Moor
      Should hazard such a place as his own second
      With one of an ingraft infirmity:
125   It were an honest action to say
      So to the Moor.

IAGO: Not I, for this fair island:
   I do love Cassio well, and would do much
   To cure him of this evil:— But, hark! What noise?
                        [A cry within, "Help, help!"]

[Reenter Cassio, driving in Roderigo.]

130 CASSIO: 'Zounds! You rogue! You rascal!

MONTANO: What's the matter, lieutenant?

CASSIO: A knave teach me my duty!
   But I'll beat the knave into a twiggen bottle.

88

MONTANO: But is he often like this?

IAGO: Almost always before he goes to bed. He'll stay awake all night if the drinking does not help him fall asleep.

MONTANO: It would be better if the general knew about this. Perhaps he does not see it, or Othello's good nature values the good side of Cassio and can not see his evil side. Is that the case?

[Enter Roderigo]

IAGO: [Aside to Roderigo] Look here, Roderigo! I beg you, go after the lieutenant. Go.   [Exit Roderigo]

MONTANO: And it is a great pity that the noble Moor should risk having as his second in command a person with such a problem. It would be an honest act to let the Moor know.

IAGO: I won't do it. I could not do that even for this fair island. I love Cassio and would do anything to cure him of this evil—But, wait! What is that noise?   [Cry from within: "Help! help!"]

[Reenter Cassio, driving in Roderigo at sword point]

CASSIO: You rogue, you rascal!

MONTANO: What's the matter, lieutenant?

CASSIO: A villain is trying to teach me my duty! I'll beat the rogue into a wicker bottle.

ROD: Beat me!

135   CASSIO: Dost thou prate, rogue?   *[Strikes Roderigo]*

MONTANO: Nay, good lieutenant; I pray you, sir, hold your hand.

CASSIO: Let me go, sir, or I'll knock you o'er the mazzard.

MONTANO: Come, come, you're drunk.

CASSIO: Drunk!   *[They fight.]*

140   IAGO: *[Aside to Roderigo]* Away, I say; go out and cry a mutiny.
        [Exit Roderigo.]

ROD: Nay, good lieutenant! God's will, gentlemen!
    Help, ho!—Lieutenant—sir—Montano sir—
    Help, masters! Here's a goodly watch indeed!   *[A bell rings.]*
    Who's that that rings the bell?—Diablo, ho!
145   The town will rise. God's will, lieutenant, hold!
    You will be shamed forever.

[Reenter Othello and Attendants.]

OTHELLO: What is the matter here?

MONTANO: 'Zounds, I bleed still; I am hurt to the death.   *[Faints.]*

OTHELLO: Hold, for your lives!

150   IAGO: Hold, ho!—Lieutenant—sir—Montano—gentlemen—
    Have you forgot all place of sense and duty?
    Hold! the general speaks to you! Hold, hold, for shame!

OTHELLO: Why, how now, ho! from whence ariseth this?
    Are we turn'd Turks, and to ourselves do that
155   Which heaven hath forbid the Ottomites?

90

ROD: [Afraid] *Beat me!*

CASSIO: *Are you babbling, rogue?* [Striking Roderigo]

MONTANO: *No, good lieutenant;* [Stopping him] *I beg you, sir, relax.*

CASSIO: *Let me go, sir, or I'll knock you over the head.*

MONTANO: *Come, come, you're drunk.*

CASSIO: *Drunk!* [They fight]

IAGO: [Aside to Roderigo] *Go away, I say; go out, and raise a commotion. Ring the alarm.* [Exit Roderigo]

ROD: [Pretending to help] *No, good lieutenant! Alas, gentlemen;—Help, ho!—Lieutenant, sir, Montano, sir; Help, masters!—This is a fine patrol I must say!* [Bell rings] *Who's that ringing the bell? The devil, ho! The town will wake up. God's will, lieutenant, stop! You will be ashamed forever.*

[Reenter Othello and Attendants]

OTHELLO: *What is the matter here?*

MONTANO: *God's wounds, I'm bleeding; I am going to die.* [Faints]

OTHELLO: *Stop right now if you want to live!*

IAGO: *Hold, ho! Lieutenant– sir—Montano,—gentlemen,—Have you forgotten your place and sense of duty? Stop it! The general speaks to you; stop, stop, for shame!*

OTHELLO: *Why, what is all of this! Where is all this coming from? Have we turned into the Turks and decided to do to ourselves what heaven has forbidden to the Ottomites? For Christian shame, put an end to this barbarous*

91

For Christian shame, put by this barbarous brawl:
He that stirs next to carve for his own rage
Holds his soul light; he dies upon his motion.
Silence that dreadful bell; it frights the isle
160   From her propriety. What is the matter, masters?
Honest Iago, that look'st dead with grieving,
Speak, who began this? On thy love, I charge thee:

IAGO: I do not know: Friends all but now, even now,
In quarter, and in terms like bride and groom
165   Devesting them for bed; and then, but now
As if some planet had unwitted men,
Swords out, and tilting one at other's breast,
In opposition bloody. I cannot speak
Any beginning to this peevish odds.

170 OTHELLO: How comes it, Michael, you are thus forgot?

CASSIO: I pray you, pardon me; I cannot speak.

OTHELLO: Worthy Montano, you were wont be civil;
The gravity and stillness of your youth
The world hath noted, and your name is great
175   In mouths of wisest censure. What's the matter,
That you unlace your reputation thus,
And spend your rich opinion for the name
Of a nightbrawler? Give me answer to it.

MONTANO: Worthy Othello, I am hurt to danger:
180   Your officer, Iago, can inform you—
While I spare speech, which something now offends me—
Of all that I do know. Nor know I aught
By me that's said or done amiss this night;
Unless self-charity be sometimes a vice,
185   And to defend ourselves it be a sin
When violence assails us.

fight. The next person that attempts to cut someone does not care about his life. He will die with his next motion. Silence that dreadful bell; it frightens the island. What is the matter, masters? Honest Iago, you look like death with grieving. Speak! Who started this? On your honor, I order you, speak.

IAGO: *I do not know. We were all friends; even now, we live in quarters with each other and are close as bride and groom; and then, but now—as if some planet had caused the men to go crazy—swords were out and thrusting at one another's breast in bloody combat. I cannot say what started this ill-natured fight.*

OTHELLO: *How did it happen, Michael; we have not heard from you.*

CASSIO: *I beg you, pardon me; I cannot speak.*

OTHELLO: *Worthy Montano, you have always been civil. Everyone knows about your seriousness and restraint, and you have a good reputation. What happened to make you undo your reputation like this and trade the good opinion others have of you to be called a night-brawler? Give me an answer.*

MONTANO: *Worthy Othello, I am really injured. Your officer, Iago, can tell you. While I try not to speak—I know that something has hurt me, and I have done nothing wrong tonight. Unless taking care of yourself is a vice, and defending yourself against violence is a sin.*

OTHELLO: Now, by heaven,
    My blood begins my safer guides to rule,
    And passion, having my best judgement collied,
190   Assays to lead the way. If I once stir,
    Or do but lift this arm, the best of you
    Shall sink in my rebuke. Give me to know
    How this foul rout began, who set it on,
    And he that is approved in this offense,
195   Though he had twinn'd with me, both at a birth,
    Shall lose me. What! in a town of war,
    Yet wild, the people's hearts brimful of fear,
    To manage private and domestic quarrel,
    In night, and on the court and guard of safety!
200   'Tis monstrous. Iago, who began't?

MONTANO: If partially affined, or leagued in office,
    Thou dost deliver more or less than truth,
    Thou art no soldier.

IAGO: Touch me not so near:
205   I had rather have this tongue cut from my mouth
    Than it should do offense to Michael Cassio;
    Yet, I persuade myself, to speak the truth
    Shall nothing wrong him. Thus it is, general.
    Montano and myself being in speech,
210   There comes a fellow crying out for help,
    And Cassio following him with determined sword,
    To execute upon him. Sir, this gentleman
    Steps in to Cassio and entreats his pause:
    Myself the crying fellow did pursue,
215   Lest by his clamor—as it so fell out—
    The town might fall in fright. He, swift of foot,
    Outran my purpose; and I return'd the rather
    For that I heard the clink and fall of swords,
    And Cassio high in oath, which till tonight
220   I ne'er might say before. When I came back—
    For this was brief—I found them close together,

OTHELLO: *Now, by heaven, my temper is beginning to overrule my reason, and passion colors my best judgment and begs to lead the way. If I make one more move, or even lift this arm, the best of you will be ruined by my reprimand. Tell me how this foul fight began and who started it. If the person who started it is found guilty, even if it was my twin brother at a birth, he will lose my love. Horrid! In a town at war, still wild, still with the people's hearts full of fear, for someone to begin a private and domestic quarrel, at night, and when on the patrol that is meant to ensure safety! It is monstrous. Iago, who started it?*

MONTANO: *[To Iago] If your relationship with Cassio makes you tell more or less than the truth, you are no soldier.*

IAGO: *Don't attack something so dear to me. I would rather have my tongue cut from my mouth than to have it offend Michael Cassio. Yet, I tell myself that if I speak the truth, I shall not wrong him. Here it is, in general. Montano and I were talking when a fellow ran by crying for help; Cassio followed the man with his sword, determined to use it. Sir, this gentleman, Montano, steps to Cassio, and begs him to stop. I myself chased the crying fellow so that his racket—as he ran around—would not frighten the town. He, being quick, outran me. And I returned here, for I heard the clash of swords and Cassio shouting oaths, which, until tonight, I have never spoken before. When I came back, I found them exchanging blows and thrusts, just as they were when you yourself separated them. I cannot report any more of this matter, except to say that men are men; the best men sometimes forget. Although Cassio did some wrong to Roderigo, as men in rage strike those that wish them best, I do believe that Cassio received some strange insult from that man who fled–this Cassio's patience could not allow.*

At blow and thrust, even as again they were
When you yourself did part them.
More of this matter cannot I report.
225   But men are men; the best sometimes forget:
Though Cassio did some little wrong to him,
As men in rage strike those that wish them best,
Yet surely Cassio, I believe, received
From him that fled some strange indignity,
230   Which patience could not pass.

OTHELLO: I know, Iago,
Thy honesty and love doth mince this matter,
Making it light to Cassio. Cassio, I love thee;
But never more be officer of mine.

[Reenter Desdemona, attended.]
235   Look, if my gentle love be not raised up!
I'll make thee an example.

DESD: What's the matter?

OTHELLO: All's well now, sweeting; come away to bed. Sir, for your
hurts, myself will be your surgeon. Lead him off.
[Exit Montano, attended].
Iago, look with care about the town,
240   And silence those whom this vile brawl distracted.
Come, Desdemona, 'tis the soldiers' life—
To have their balmy slumbers waked with strife.
[Exeunt all but Iago and Cassio]

IAGO: What, are you hurt, lieutenant?

CASSIO: Ay, past all surgery.

245   IAGO: Marry, heaven forbid!

CASSIO: Reputation, reputation, reputation! O, I have lost my

OTHELLO: *I know, Iago, your honesty and love make less of what has happened, making it easier on Cassio. Cassio, I love you, but you will never again be my second in command.*

[Reenter Desdemona, attended]
Look, my gentle love was awakened! I will make an example out of you.

DESD: *What's the matter?*

OTHELLO: *All's well now, sweetness; come away to bed.* [To Montano, who is led off] *Sir, for your injuries, I will be your surgeon. Lead him away.* [Exit Montano, attended] *Iago, look carefully around the town and quiet the people who were distracted by this shameful brawl. Come, Desdemona, it is the soldiers' life to have their sweet slumbers awakened with conflict.*
[Exit all but Iago and Cassio]

IAGO: *Are you hurt, lieutenant?*

CASSIO: *Yes, not even surgery can help me now.*

IAGO: *Oh my, heaven forbid!*

CASSIO: *Reputation, reputation, reputation! Oh, I have lost my reputation! I*

reputation! I have lost the immortal part of myself, and what remains is bestial. My reputation, Iago, my reputation!

IAGO: As I am an honest man, I thought you had received some bodily
250 wound; there is more sense in that than in reputation. Reputation is an idle and most false imposition; oft got without merit and lost without deserving. You have lost no reputation at all, unless you repute yourself such a loser. What, man! there are ways to recover the general again. You are but now cast in his mood, a punishment
255 more in policy than in malice; even so as one would beat his offenseless dog to affright an imperious lion. Sue to him again, and he's yours.

CASSIO: I will rather sue to be despised than to deceive so good a commander with so slight, so drunken, and so indiscreet an officer.
260 Drunk? and speak parrot? and squabble? swagger? swear? and discourse fustian with one's own shadow? O thou invisible spirit of wine, if thou hast no name to be known by, let us call thee devil!

IAGO: What was he that you followed with your sword? What had he done to you?

265 CASSIO: I know not.

IAGO: Is't possible?

CASSIO: I remember a mass of things, but nothing distinctly; a quarrel, but nothing wherefore. O God, that men should put an enemy in their mouths to steal away their brains! that we should, with joy,
270 pleasance, revel, and applause, transform ourselves into beasts!

IAGO: Why, but you are now well enough. How came you thus recovered?

CASSIO: It hath pleased the devil drunkenness to give place to the devil wrath: one unperfectness shows me another, to make me frankly
275 despise myself.

have lost the immortal part of myself, and only my inner beast remains. My reputation, Iago, my reputation!

IAGO: Being that I am an honest man, I thought you meant you had received some bodily wound. Crying for a wound would make more sense than crying about your reputation. Reputation is a worthless and misleading thing. Often it is won without earning it and lost without deserving to lose it. You have lost no reputation at all, unless you think of yourself as such a loser. Listen, man! There are ways to win back the general again. You are now cast down because the general is in a bad mood; it is a punishment given more because of policy than of hatred. Just like someone beating his innocent dog to frighten an arrogant lion. Make your case to him again, and he'll reconsider.

CASSIO: I would rather he despise me than to trick such a good commander as Othello into being served by an officer so stupid, so drunken, and so indiscreet: Drunk? Speak nonsense? Fight? Stumble? Swear? Converse with one's own shadow? Oh, you invisible spirit of wine, if you have no name to be known by, let us call you the devil!

IAGO: Who was the man that you followed with your sword? What did he do to you?

CASSIO: I don't know.

IAGO: Is it possible?

CASSIO: I remember a lot, but nothing exact. There was a fight, but I remember nothing else. Oh, God, that men should put an enemy in their mouths that steals their brains! And that we should, with joy, enjoy, applause, and transform ourselves into beasts!

IAGO: You seem fine now. How did you recover so quickly?

CASSIO: It has pleased the devil of drunkenness to leave, giving the stage to the devil of anger. One imperfection leads to another and makes me honestly hate myself.

99

IAGO: Come, you are too severe a moraler. As the time, the place, and the condition of this country stands, I could heartily wish this had not befallen; but since it is as it is, mend it for your own good.

CASSIO: I will ask him for my place again; he shall tell me I am a
280   drunkard! Had I as many mouths as Hydra, such an answer would stop them all. To be now a sensible man, by and by a fool, and presently a beast! O strange! Every inordinate cup is unblest, and the ingredient is a devil.

IAGO: Come, come, good wine is a good familiar creature, if it be well
285   used. Exclaim no more against it. And, good lieutenant, I think you think I love you.

CASSIO: I have well approved it, sir. I drunk!

IAGO: You or any man living may be drunk at some time, man. I'll tell you what you shall do. Our general's wife is now the general. I may
290   say so in this respect, for that he hath devoted and given up himself to the contemplation, mark, and denotement of her parts and graces. Confess yourself freely to her; importune her help to put you in your place again. She is of so free, so kind, so apt, so blessed a disposition, she holds it a vice in her goodness not to do more
295   than she is requested. This broken joint between you and her husband entreat her to splinter; and, my fortunes against any lay worth naming, this crack of your love shall grow stronger than it was before.

CASSIO: You advise me well.

300 IAGO: I protest, in the sincerity of love and honest kindness.

CASSIO: I think it freely; and betimes in the morning I will beseech the virtuous Desdemona to undertake for me. I am desperate of my fortunes if they check me here.

IAGO: You are in the right. Good night, lieutenant, I must to the watch.

IAGO: Come, you are too hard on yourself. With the state that this country is in, I sincerely wish that all this had not happened, but since it has, you must learn from it.

CASSIO: I will ask the general for my position again; he will tell me I am a drunkard! And if I had as many mouths as Hydra, that answer would shut them all. To be at one moment a sensible man, the next moment a fool, and then a beast! Oh, it is strange! Every excessive cup of wine is a sin, and the ingredient is a devil.

IAGO: Come, come, good wine can be a good friend, if it is used wisely. Don't say anything else bad about it. And, good lieutenant, I think you know I am devoted to you.

CASSIO: I have earned your respect, sir. I am a drunk!

IAGO: You or any man living may get drunk at some time! I'll tell you what you should do. Our general's wife is now in charge. What I mean is that the general has devoted himself to the contemplation, attention, and study of her body and charm. Confess your guilt freely to her, and ask her to help you regain your position. She is free, kind, and competent; she has a blessed temperament, and she thinks that it is a weakness in her goodness not to do more than is requested of her. Get her to mend the wound between you and her husband. I'll bet my fortunes against anything you want to name that she will mend the crack in your love, and it will grow stronger than it was before.

CASSIO: You have given me good advice.

IAGO: In all sincerity and honest kindness, I am just trying to help.

CASSIO: I will think more about this on my own. In the morning I will ask the virtuous Desdemona to help me. I am desperate about my future if my career ends here.

IAGO: You are in the right. Good night, lieutenant; I must go on patrol.

305   CASSIO: Good night, honest Iago.   *[Exit.]*

      IAGO: And what's he then that says I play the villain?
          When this advice is free I give and honest,
          Probal to thinking, and indeed the course
          To win the Moor again? For 'tis most easy
310   The inclining Desdemona to subdue
          In any honest suit. She's framed as fruitful
          As the free elements. And then for her
          To win the Moor, were't to renounce his baptism,
          All seals and symbols of redeemed sin,
315   His soul is so enfetter'd to her love,
          That she may make, unmake, do what she list,
          Even as her appetite shall play the god
          With his weak function. How am I then a villain
          To counsel Cassio to this parallel course,
320   Directly to his good? Divinity of hell!
          When devils will the blackest sins put on,
          They do suggest at first with heavenly shows,
          As I do now. For whiles this honest fool
          Plies Desdemona to repair his fortune,
325   And she for him pleads strongly to the Moor,
          I'll pour this pestilence into his ear,
          That she repeals him for her body's lust;
          And by how much she strives to do him good,
          She shall undo her credit with the Moor.
330   So will I turn her virtue into pitch,
          And out of her own goodness make the net
          That shall enmesh them all.

      [Enter Roderigo]
      How now, Roderigo!

      ROD: I do follow here in the chase, not like a hound that hunts, but
      one that fills up the cry. My money is almost spent; I have been
335   tonight exceedingly well cudgeled; and I think the issue will be, I
      shall have so much experience for my pains; and so, with no
      money at all and a little more wit, return again to Venice.

CASSIO: *Good night, honest Iago.*   [Exit]

IAGO: *And who says that I am the villain?*
Will my honest, sensible advice enable Cassio to win back the Moor's affections? It is very easy to get Desdemona to present his case. She is as generous as the world's resources. She would be able to convince the Moor of anything—she could probably get him to give up Christianity. His soul is a prisoner of her love; she could make or unmake whatever she wanted. Her desires are in full control when it comes to weak Othello. Why, then, am I a villain to counsel Cassio to try this, directly helping him? Divinity of hell! When the devil commits his blackest sin, he begins by showing kindness, as I do now. While this honest fool tries to persuade Desdemona to fix his troubles, and she pleads for him strongly to the Moor, I'll pour the poison lie into Othello's ear, that she appeals Cassio's case for her body's lust. Then, when she tries to do Cassio a favor, she shall look bad to the Moor. That's how I will turn her virtue into tar and make a net out of her own goodness that shall catch them all.

[Reenter Roderigo]
Hello, Roderigo!

ROD: *I have been chased here like a dog, not like the lead hunting hound, but like a dog at the back of the pack. My money is almost all spent, and tonight I have been severely beaten. I have to ask myself, is this worth it? I will return to Venice with no money at all, and only a little more common sense.*

IAGO: How poor are they that have not patience!
    What wound did ever heal but by degrees?
340   Thou know'st we work by wit and not by witchcraft,
    And wit depends on dilatory time.
    Does't not go well? Cassio hath beaten thee,
    And thou by that small hurt hast cashier'd Cassio
    Though other things grow fair against the sun,
345   Yet fruits that blossom first will first be ripe:
    Content thyself awhile. By the mass, 'tis morning;
    Pleasure and action make the hours seem short.
    Retire thee; go where thou art billeted:
    Away, I say. Thou shalt know more hereafter:
350   Nay, get thee gone.   *[Exit Roderigo]*
    Two things are to be done:
    My wife must move for Cassio to her mistress;
    I'll set her on;
    Myself the while to draw the Moor apart,
355   And bring him jump when he may Cassio find
    Soliciting his wife: Ay, that's the way;
    Dull not device by coldness and delay.

                              [Exit.]

IAGO: *How poor are the people who have no patience! When did an injury ever heal except with time and patience? You know we work by intellect and reason, and not by witchcraft. Intelligent plans depend on unhurried time. Isn't everything going well? Cassio has beaten you. And you, because of that small injury, have gotten Cassio discharged from his position. All things grow beautiful in the sun, but the fruits that blossom first, will ripen first. Be patient awhile. It is morning. All of this fun and excitement make the hours seem short. Get some sleep. Go home. Go, I say. You will know more later. Now, get going.* [Exit Roderigo] *Two things have to be done: My wife must put in a good word for Cassio with Desdemona. I'll get her to do that. In the meantime, I will work on the Moor. I'll get him to come around at just the right time to find Cassio approaching his wife. Yes, that's the plan; I must not ruin the plan with indifference or hesitation.*

[Exit]

ACT III

SCENE 1
Before the castle.

[Enter Cassio and some Musicians.]

CASSIO: Masters, play here, I will content your pains; Something that's brief; and bid "Good morrow, general." *[Music.]*

[Enter Clown.]

CLOWN. Why, masters, have your instruments been in Naples, that they speak i' the nose thus?

5   FIRST MUSICIAN. How, sir, how?

CLOWN. Are these, I pray you, wind instruments?

FIRST MUSICIAN: Ay, marry, are they, sir.

CLOWN: O, thereby hangs a tail.

FIRST MUSICIAN: Whereby hangs a tale, sir?

10   CLOWN: Marry, sir. But, masters, here's money for you; and the general so likes your music, that he desires you, for love's sake, to make no more noise with it.

FIRST MUSICIAN. Well, sir, we will not.

ACT III

SCENE 1
In front of the castle.

[Enter Cassio and some Musicians]

CASSIO:Musicians, play here. I will pay you. Play something that's brief, and says "Good morning, general." [Music]

[Enter Clown]

CLOWN: Why, masters, have your instruments been in Naples, that they speak through the nose like that?

FIRST MUSICIAN: What, sir?

CLOWN: I wonder, are these wind instruments?

FIRST MUSICIAN: Yes, sir, they are.

CLOWN: Oh, there's a tale hanging on that.

FIRST MUSICIAN: By which hangs a tale, sir?

CLOWN: I agree, sir, with many wind instruments. But, masters, here's money for you. The general loves your music so much that he wants you, for love's sake, to make no more noise with it.

FIRST MUSICIAN: Well, sir, we will not.

CLOWN: If you have any music that may not be heard, to't again; but,
15   as they say, to hear music the general does not greatly care.

FIRST MUSICIAN: We have none such, sir.

CLOWN: Then put up your pipes in your bag, for I'll away. Go, vanish
into air, away!   *[Exeunt Musicians.]*

CASSIO: Dost thou hear, my honest friend?

20   CLOWN: No, I hear not your honest friend; I hear you.

CASSIO: Prithee, keep up thy quillets. There's a poor piece of gold for
thee. If the gentlewoman that attends the general's wife be stirring,
tell her there's one Cassio entreats her a little favor of speech. Wilt
thou do this?

25   CLOWN: She is stirring, sir. If she will stir hither, I shall seem to notify
unto her.

CASSIO: Do, good my friend.   *[Exit Clown]*

[Enter Iago.]
     In happy time, Iago

IAGO: You have not been abed, then?

30   CASSIO: Why, no; the day had broke
     Before we parted. I have made bold, Iago,
     To send in to your wife. My suit to her
     Is that she will to virtuous Desdemona
     Procure me some access.

35   IAGO: I'll send her to you presently;
     And I'll devise a mean to draw the Moor
     Out of the way, that your converse and business
     May be more free.

CLOWN: *If you have any silent music you could play, then go ahead and play it. But, as they say, the general is not really interested in music with notes.*

FIRST MUSICIAN: *We have no silent music, sir.*

CLOWN: *Then put away your pipes, and get going. Go, vanish into the air; away!*   [Exit Musicians]

CASSIO: *Do you hear, my honest friend?*

CLOWN: *No, I don't hear your honest friend; I hear you.*

CASSIO: *Please keep on making your wisecracks. I'll pay you a small piece of gold. If the gentlewoman that attends the general's wife is awake, tell her that Cassio is here, who would like to speak to her. Will you do this?*

CLOWN: *She is awake, sir. If she will be awake here, I will appear to ask her.*

CASSIO: *Do, my good friend.*   [Exit Clown]

[Enter Iago]
    You got here at a good time, Iago.

IAGO: *You have not been to bed, then?*

CASSIO: *Why, no; the sun had come up before we parted. I have made a bold move, Iago, by sending a message to your wife. I intend to see if she can get virtuous Desdemona to speak with me.*

IAGO: *I'll send my wife to you right away, and I'll think of an excuse to get the Moor out of the way, so your conversation and business with Desdemona may be more open.*

CASSIO: I humbly thank you for't. [Exit Iago] I never knew
40   A Florentine more kind and honest.

[Enter Emilia.]

EMILIA: Good morrow, good lieutenant. I am sorry
      For your displeasure, but all will sure be well.
      The general and his wife are talking of it,
      And she speaks for you stoutly. The Moor replies
45   That he you hurt is of great fame in Cyprus
      And great affinity and that in wholesome wisdom
      He might not but refuse you; but he protests he loves you,
      And needs no other suitor but his likings
      To take the safest occasion by the front
50   To bring you in again.

CASSIO: Yet, I beseech you,
      If you think fit, or that it may be done,
      Give me advantage of some brief discourse
      With Desdemona alone.

55 EMILIA: Pray you, come in.
      I will bestow you where you shall have time
      To speak your bosom freely.

CASSIO: I am much bound to you.

                                [Exeunt]

CASSIO: *I humbly thank you for your help.* [Exit Iago] *I never knew a person from Florence to be more kind and honest than Iago.*

[Enter Emilia]

EMILIA: *Good morning, good lieutenant. I am sorry about your situation, but everything will work out. The general and his wife are talking about it right now, and she defends you vigorously. The Moor replies that the man you hurt, Montano, is famous and well-loved in Cyprus, and the wise thing for him would be to refuse your request for a second chance. But then the Moor declares that he loves you, and that he needs no other person to persuade him that he should, at a safe time, bring you in again to give you a second chance.*

CASSIO: *I beg you; if you think it is right, or that it is possible, please give me the opportunity to speak briefly with Desdemona alone.*

EMILIA: *Please, come in. I will put you where you will have some time to say freely what is in your heart.*

CASSIO: *I am in debt to you.* [Exeunt]

SCENE 2
A room in the castle.

[Enter Othello, Iago, and Gentlemen.]

OTHELLO: These letters give, Iago, to the pilot;
  And by him do my duties to the Senate:
  That done, I will be walking on the works;
  Repair there to me.

5 IAGO: Well, my good lord, I'll do't.

OTHELLO: This fortification, gentlemen, shall we see't?

GENTLEMEN: We'll wait upon your lordship.
          [Exeunt.]

SCENE 3
The garden of the castle.

[Enter Desdemona, Cassio, and Emilia.]

DESD: Be thou assured, good Cassio, I will do
  All my abilities in thy behalf.

EMILIA: Good madam, do: I warrant it grieves my husband
  As if the cause were his.

5 DESD: O, that's an honest fellow. Do not doubt, Cassio,
  But I will have my lord and you again
  As friendly as you were.

CASSIO: Bounteous madam,
  Whatever shall become of Michael Cassio,
10 He's never anything but your true servant.

112

SCENE 2
A room in the castle.

[Enter Othello, Iago, and Gentlemen]

OTHELLO: *Iago, give these letters to the ship's captain, and have him report to the Senate for me. When that is done, I will be walking around checking the castle walls. Come see me there.*

IAGO: *Yes, my good lord, I will do it.*

OTHELLO: *Shall we inspect the defensive barrier, gentlemen?*

GENTLEMAN: *We will accompany your lordship.*

[Exeunt]

SCENE 3
The garden of the castle.

[Enter Desdemona, Cassio, and Emilia]

DESD: *You can be assured, good Cassio, I will do everything within my power to help you.*

EMILIA: *Good madam, please do. I guarantee you that it hurts my husband as if this problem were his own.*

DESD: *Oh, that Iago is an honest fellow. Cassio, don't worry, I will make sure that you and my lord will become friends again, as you were before.*

CASSIO: *Gracious madam, whatever happens to Michael Cassio, he will always be a faithful servant to you.*

DESD: I know't: I thank you. You do love my lord:
    You have known him long; and be you well assured
    He shall in strangeness stand no farther off
    Than in a politic distance.

15 CASSIO: Ay, but, lady,
    That policy may either last so long,
    Or feed upon such nice and waterish diet,
    Or breed itself so out of circumstances,
    That I being absent and my place supplied,
20   My general will forget my love and service.

DESD: Do not doubt that. Before Emilia here
    I give thee warrant of thy place, assure thee,
    If I do vow a friendship, I'll perform it
    To the last article. My lord shall never rest;
25   I'll watch him tame and talk him out of patience;
    His bed shall seem a school, his board a shrift;
    I'll intermingle everything he does
    With Cassio's suit. Therefore be merry, Cassio,
    For thy solicitor shall rather die
30   Than give thy cause away.

[Enter Othello and Iago, at a distance.]

EMILIA: Madam, here comes my lord.

CASSIO: Madam, I'll take my leave.

DESD: Nay, stay and hear me speak.

CASSIO: Madam, not now. I am very ill at ease,
35   Unfit for mine own purposes.

DESD: Well, do your discretion.   *[Exit Cassio.]*

[Enter Othello and Iago.]

DESD: I know that, and I thank you. You love my lord, and you have known him a long time. Rest assured that if he pushes you aside, it will be no farther than is necessary for the sake of appearances.

CASSIO: Yes, lady, but his anger may last so long, become easy and pleasant for him to live with, or it may become a habit. If that happens, my absence– and my position being filled–will cause Othello to forget my love and services.

DESD: Do not be afraid of that. In front of Emilia here, I guarantee you your position. You may rest assured that if I vow to perform a favor, I'll do it. I'll make your case at all times. My lord will never rest without hearing about it. I'll watch him and I'll talk to him until he loses patience. His bed will seem like a school and his dinner table a confessional. I'll mix Cassio's case into everything Othello does; therefore, be happy, Cassio, because your lawyer would rather die than let you down.

[Enter Othello and Iago, at a distance]

EMILIA: Madam, here comes my lord.

CASSIO: Madam, I must go.

DESD: No, stay, and hear me speak.

CASSIO: Madam, not now. I am very uncomfortable, and it would not help my case if I stayed.

DESD: Well, it is up to you.   [Exit Cassio]

[Enter Othello and Iago]

IAGO: Ha! I like not that.

OTHELLO: What dost thou say?

IAGO: Nothing, my lord; or if I know not what.

40   OTHELLO: Was not that Cassio parted from my wife?

IAGO: Cassio, my lord! No, sure, I cannot think it,
    That he would steal away so guiltylike,
    Seeing you coming.

OTHELLO: I do believe 'twas he.

45   DESD: How now, my lord!
        I have been talking with a suitor here,
        A man that languishes in your displeasure.

OTHELLO: Who is't you mean?

DESD: Why, your lieutenant, Cassio. Good my lord,
50   If I have any grace or power to move you,
        His present reconciliation take;
        For if he be not one that truly loves you,
        That errs in ignorance and not in cunning,
        I have no judgement in an honest face:
55   I prithee, call him back.

OTHELLO: Went he hence now?

DESD: Ay, sooth; so humbled,
        That he hath left part of his grief with me,
        To suffer with him. Good love, call him back.

60   OTHELLO: Not now, sweet Desdemona; some other time.

DESD: But shall't be shortly?

116

IAGO: Ha! I don't like that.

OTHELLO: What did you say?

IAGO: Nothing, my lord, or if—I don't know.

OTHELLO: Wasn't that Cassio who just left my wife?

IAGO: Cassio, my lord! No, surely, I can't imagine Cassio would slip away looking guilty after seeing you coming.

OTHELLO: I do believe that it was Cassio.

DESD: How are you, my lord? I have been talking with a petitioner, a man who wastes away because you are unhappy with him.

OTHELLO: Who do you mean?

DESD: Why, your lieutenant, Cassio. My lord, if I have power to convince you, please accept his apology. Because if he is not a man who truly loves you, who has made an honest mistake, not a planned one, then I cannot tell an honest face. I beg you, call him back.

OTHELLO: Was that Cassio who just left?

DESD: Yes, and honestly, he is so ashamed that he has left part of his grief with me, and now I suffer with him. Good love, call him back.

OTHELLO: Not now, sweet Desdemona; some other time.

DESD: Will it be soon?

OTHELLO: The sooner, sweet, for you.

DESD: Shall't be tonight at supper?

OTHELLO: No, not tonight.

65 DESD: Tomorrow dinner then?

OTHELLO: I shall not dine at home;
    I meet the captains at the citadel.

DESD: Why then tomorrow night, or Tuesday morn;
    On Tuesday noon, or night, on Wednesday morn;
70   I prithee, name the time, but let it not
    Exceed three days. In faith, he's penitent;
    And yet his trespass, in our common reason—
    Save that, they say, the wars must make examples
    Out of their best—is not almost a fault
75   To incur a private check. When shall he come?
    Tell me, Othello I wonder in my soul,
    What you would ask me, that I should deny,
    Or stand so mammering on. What? Michael Cassio,
    That came awooing with you, and so many a time
80   When I have spoke of you dispraisingly
    Hath ta'en your part to have so much to do
    To bring him in! Trust me, I could do much—

OTHELLO: Prithee, no more. Let him come when he will;
    I will deny thee nothing.

85 DESD: Why, this is not a boon;
    'Tis as I should entreat you wear your gloves,
    Or feed on nourishing dishes, or keep you warm,
    Or sue to you to do a peculiar profit
    To your own person. Nay, when I have a suit
90   Wherein I mean to touch your love indeed,
    It shall be full of poise and difficult weight,
    And fearful to be granted.

OTHELLO: *Sooner for you, my sweet.*

DESD: *Will it be tonight at supper?*

OTHELLO: *No, not tonight.*

DESD: *Tomorrow at dinner, then?*

OTHELLO: *I will not be eating at home. I must meet the captains at the castle.*

DESD: *Why, then, tomorrow night, or Tuesday morning, Tuesday noon, or night, or even Wednesday morning. I beg you, name the time, but do not let it be more than three days. I swear, he is sorry. And yet his mistake, as we see it—except they say that wars create examples out of their heroes—it is hardly a fault that deserves to be reprimanded privately. When should he come to speak with you? Tell me, Othello. My conscience is curious. What demand could you make of me that I would deny or hesitate about. What? Michael Cassio, who came with you to court me and who defended you on many occasions when I said insulting things about you, took your side—And you don't have time to meet with him! Trust me, I could do so much—*

OTHELLO: *Please, no more. Let him come whenever he wants. I will deny you nothing.*

DESD: *Why, this is not a favor for me. You act like I'm trying to get you to wear your gloves, eat your vegetables, keep warm, or beg you to make a personal improvement. No, when I need something, and I try to touch your heart, it will be important, difficult, and dangerous to grant.*

OTHELLO: I will deny thee nothing:
    Whereon, I do beseech thee, grant me this,
95   To leave me but a little to myself.

DESD: Shall I deny you? No. Farewell, my lord.

OTHELLO: Farewell, my Desdemona; I'll come to thee straight.

DESD: Emilia, come. Be as your fancies teach you; Whate'er you be, I
    am obedient.   *[Exeunt Desdemona and Emilia.]*

100 OTHELLO: Excellent wretch! Perdition catch my soul,
    But I do love thee! and when I love thee not,
    Chaos is come again.

IAGO: My noble lord—

OTHELLO: What dost thou say, Iago?

IAGO: Did Michael Cassio, when you woo'd my lady,
105   Know of your love?

OTHELLO: He did, from first to last. Why dost thou ask?

IAGO: But for a satisfaction of my thought;
    No further harm.

OTHELLO: Why of thy thought, Iago?

110 IAGO: I did not think he had been acquainted with her.

OTHELLO: O, yes, and went between us very oft.

IAGO: Indeed!

OTHELLO: Indeed? ay, indeed. Discern'st thou aught in that?
115   Is he not honest?

OTHELLO: *I will never say no to you. So, please do just one thing for me: leave me alone right now.*

DESD: *Will I ever say no to you? No. Goodbye, my lord.*

OTHELLO: *Farewell, my Desdemona. I'll be with you soon.*

DESD: *Emilia, come. You may be whatever you like, but as for me, I am obedient.*   [Exit Desdemona and Emilia]

OTHELLO: [Thinking aloud of Desdemona] *Excellent woman! Damn my soul, but I do love you, and when I stop loving you, chaos will come again.*

IAGO: *My noble lord*—

OTHELLO: *What do you say, Iago?*

IAGO: *Did Michael Cassio know about your love when you wooed your lady?*

OTHELLO: *He did, from the beginning. Why do you ask?*

IAGO: *Only out of curiosity; it's nothing really.*

OTHELLO: *What are you curious about, Iago?*

IAGO: *I did not think he knew her.*

OTHELLO: *Oh, yes; and he served as our messenger often.*

IAGO: *Indeed!*

OTHELLO: *Indeed! Yes, indeed. Do you see something in that? Is he honest?*

IAGO: Honest, my lord?

OTHELLO: Honest? Ay, honest.

IAGO: My lord, for aught I know.

OTHELLO: What dost thou think?

120 IAGO: Think, my lord?

OTHELLO: Think, my lord? By heaven, he echoes me,
      As if there were some monster in his thought
      Too hideous to be shown. Thou dost mean something:
      I heard thee say even now, thou like'st not that,
125   When Cassio left my wife. What didst not like?
      And when I told thee he was of my counsel
      In my whole course of wooing, thou criedst, "Indeed!"
      And didst contract and purse thy brow together,
      As if thou then hadst shut up in thy brain
130   Some horrible conceit. If thou dost love me,
      Show me thy thought.

IAGO: My lord, you know I love you.

OTHELLO: I think thou dost;
      And for I know thou'rt full of love and honesty
135   And weigh'st thy words before thou givest them breath,
      Therefore these stops of thine fright me the more;
      For such things in a false disloyal knave
      Are tricks of custom; but in a man that's just
      They're close dilations, working from the heart,
140   That passion cannot rule.

IAGO: For Michael Cassio,
      I dare be sworn I think that he is honest.

OTHELLO: I think so too.

IAGO: Honest, my lord?

OTHELLO: Honest? Yes, honest.

IAGO: My lord, I know nothing about it.

OTHELLO: What do you think?

IAGO: Think, my lord?

OTHELLO: [Mocking] Think, my lord? By heaven, he echoes me, as if there is some terrible monster hidden in his thought too hideous to reveal. You do mean something. I heard you say, when Cassio left my wife, that you didn't like it. What didn't you like? And when I told you he was my messenger in my course of wooing, you cried 'Indeed!' You wrinkled your eyes and made a face, as if you had to lock some terrible thought in your brain. If you do love me, tell me what you are thinking.

IAGO: My lord, you know I love you.

OTHELLO: I think you do. And I know you are full of love and honesty, and I know you think about what you are going to say before you say it. Therefore, the way you keep pausing scares me even more. Such things in a false, disloyal knave are tricks of habit, but in an honest man, they are secret emotions from the heart, which cannot be concealed.

IAGO: As for Michael Cassio, I swear that he is honest.

OTHELLO: I think so too.

123

IAGO: Men should be what they seem;
145   Or those that be not, would they might seem none!

OTHELLO: Certain, men should be what they seem.

IAGO: Why then I think Cassio's an honest man.

OTHELLO: Nay, yet there's more in this:
       I prithee, speak to me as to thy thinkings,
150   As thou dost ruminate, and give thy worst of thoughts
       The worst of words.

IAGO: Good my lord, pardon me;
       Though I am bound to every act of duty,
       I am not bound to that all slaves are free to.
155   Utter my thoughts? Why, say they are vile and false;
       As where's that palace whereinto foul things
       Sometimes intrude not? Who has a breast so pure,
       But some uncleanly apprehensions
       Keep leets and lawdays, and in session sit
160   With meditations lawful?

OTHELLO: Thou dost conspire against thy friend, Iago,
       If thou but think'st him wrong'd and makest his ear
       A stranger to thy thoughts.

IAGO: I do beseech you—
165   Though I perchance am vicious in my guess,
       As, I confess, it is my nature's plague
       To spy into abuses, and oft my jealousy
       Shapes faults that are not—that your wisdom yet,
       From one that so imperfectly conceits,
170   Would take no notice, nor build yourself a trouble
       Out of his scattering and unsure observance.
       It were not for your quiet nor your good,
       Nor for my manhood, honesty, or wisdom,
       To let you know my thoughts.

IAGO: Men should be what they appear to be; those that are not, I wish would not appear to be men.

OTHELLO: Absolutely, men should be what they appear to be.

IAGO: Why, then, I think Cassio is an honest man.

OTHELLO: No, but there is more to this. I beg you, tell me what you are thinking as you think it, and give your worst thoughts the worst words.

IAGO: Good my lord, excuse me. Even though I am bound to do my duty, I am not bound to reveal my thoughts; even slaves are free not to do that. Express my thoughts? What if they are evil and false? Don't foul and dirty things sometimes intrude even into a palace? Who has a heart so pure that he does not have some immoral suspicions that sit next to his honest thoughts when he is making judgements?

OTHELLO: You plot against your friend, Iago, if you think he has been wronged and do not tell him what you think.

IAGO: I beg of you, though my suspicion may be evil—I admit that it is my nature to sometimes see wrongs that are not real, and often my jealousy creates crimes that are not true— it is not in your best interest for you to hear these vague thoughts, these scattered and unreliable observations. It's not for your own good or for your peace of mind, nor for my manhood, honesty, or wisdom to let you know my thoughts.

175   OTHELLO: What dost thou mean?

     IAGO: Good name in man and woman, dear my lord,
        Is the immediate jewel of their souls:
        Who steals my purse steals trash; 'tis something, nothing;
        'Twas mine, 'tis his, and has been slave to thousands;
180   But he that filches from me my good name
        Robs me of that which not enriches him
        And makes me poor indeed.

     OTHELLO: By heaven, I'll know thy thoughts.

     IAGO: You cannot, if my heart were in your hand;
185   Nor shall not, whilst 'tis in my custody.

     OTHELLO: Ha!

     IAGO: O, beware, my lord, of jealousy!
        It is the greeneyed monster, which doth mock
        The meat it feeds on. That cuckold lives in bliss
190   Who, certain of his fate, loves not his wronger;
        But O, what damned minutes tells he o'er
        Who dotes, yet doubts, suspects, yet strongly loves!

     OTHELLO: O misery!

     IAGO: Poor and content is rich, and rich enough;
195   But riches fineless is as poor as winter
        To him that ever fears he shall be poor.
        Good heaven, the souls of all my tribe defend
        From jealousy!

     OTHELLO: Why, why is this?
200   Think'st thou I'd make a life of jealousy,
        To follow still the changes of the moon
        With fresh suspicions? No! To be once in doubt
        Is once to be resolved. Exchange me for a goat,

OTHELLO: *What do you mean?*

IAGO: *A man or woman's good name, my dear lord, is the most valuable jewel in their souls. Whoever steals my wallet steals trash. Money is something, then suddenly nothing. It was mine, now it is his, and has belonged to thousands before us. But the person who steals my good name from me robs me of something that cannot make him any richer, yet makes me poor indeed.*

OTHELLO: *By God, I will know your thoughts.*

IAGO: *You cannot, even if you held my heart in your hand; nor will you hear them while my heart is in my possession.*

OTHELLO: *Ha!*

IAGO: *Oh, my lord, beware of jealousy. It is the green-eyed monster that mocks the person it feeds on. The man whose wife has been unfaithful lives happily as long as he does not love his wife. But, oh, what a hellish life a man lives when he pampers and loves his wife deeply, yet also doubts and suspects her.*

OTHELLO: *Oh, misery!*

IAGO: *To be poor and content is like being rich enough. But endless riches bring little happiness to a man who lives in fear that he shall be poor. Good heaven, defend the souls of my family from jealousy!*

OTHELLO: *Why, why do you say this? Do you think I would live a life of jealousy, changing suspicions as often as the moon changes? No! A person may have doubt, but then it must be resolved. Exchange me for a goat, when I begin to spend time making overblown theories that match what you imply. It does not make me jealous if one says that my wife is pretty, a good cook,*

127

When I shall turn the business of my soul
205　　To such exsufflicate and blown surmises,
Matching thy inference. 'Tis not to make me jealous
To say my wife is fair, feeds well, loves company,
Is free of speech, sings, plays, and dances well;
Where virtue is, these are more virtuous.
210　　Nor from mine own weak merits will I draw
The smallest fear or doubt of her revolt;
For she had eyes and chose me.
No, Iago, I'll see before I doubt; when I doubt, prove;
And on the proof, there is no more but this,
215　　Away at once with love or jealousy!

IAGO: I am glad of it, for now I shall have reason
To show the love and duty that I bear you
With franker spirit. Therefore, as I am bound,
Receive it from me. I speak not yet of proof.
220　　Look to your wife; observe her well with Cassio;
Wear your eye thus, not jealous nor secure.
I would not have your free and noble nature
Out of selfbounty be abused. Look to't.
I know our country disposition well;
225　　In Venice they do let heaven see the pranks
They dare not show their husbands; their best conscience
Is not to leave't undone, but keep't unknown.

OTHELLO: Dost thou say so?

IAGO: She did deceive her father, marrying you;
230　　And when she seem'd to shake and fear your looks,
She loved them most.

OTHELLO: And so she did.

IAGO: Why, go to then.
She that so young could give out such a seeming,
235　　To seel her father's eyes up close as oak—

loves company, speaks her mind, sings, plays, and dances well. Where there are impressive qualities, these are more praiseworthy. Nor will I worry about her leaving me, for my lack of self-worth, because she had eyes, and she chose me. No, Iago, I will see, before I doubt. When I doubt, I will look for proof, and if there is proof, then that is that. To hell with love or jealousy!

IAGO: I am glad to hear it, because now I have a reason to show the love and duty that I have for you with an open spirit. Therefore, because I am so devoted to you, take this from me. I do not have proof. Watch your wife; observe her with Cassio. Do not be jealous or unsuspecting either; I would not like to see your free and noble nature, abused because of your own generosity. Watch them. I know what people from Venice are like; they let heaven see the deeds that they do not dare show their husbands. Their way of living is to commit the deed, but keep it secret.

OTHELLO: You think so?

IAGO: Desdemona deceived her father to marry you. When she pretended to fear you, she actually loved you.

OTHELLO: Yes, she did.

IAGO: Why, it's obvious. She, so young, could act well enough to keep her father blind—he thought it was witchcraft. I deserve a lot of the blame; I humbly ask you to excuse me for loving you too much.

129

He thought 'twas witchcraft—but I am much to blame;
I humbly do beseech you of your pardon
For too much loving you.

OTHELLO: I am bound to thee forever.

240 IAGO: I see this hath a little dash'd your spirits.

OTHELLO: Not a jot, not a jot.

IAGO: I'faith, I fear it has.
    I hope you will consider what is spoke
    Comes from my love. But I do see you're moved;
245   I am to pray you not to strain my speech
    To grosser issues, nor to larger reach
    Than to suspicion.

OTHELLO: I will not.

IAGO: Should you do so, my lord,
250   My speech should fall into such vile success
    Which my thoughts aim not at. Cassio's my worthy friend—
    My lord, I see you're moved.

OTHELLO: No, not much moved.
    I do not think but Desdemona's honest.

255 IAGO: Long live she so! and long live you to think so!

OTHELLO: And yet, how nature erring from itself—

IAGO: Ay, there's the point, as—to be bold with you—
    Not to affect many proposed matches
    Of her own clime, complexion, and degree,
260   Whereto we see in all things nature tends—
    Foh, one may smell in such a will most rank,

130

OTHELLO: I am bound to you forever.

IAGO: I see this has upset you a bit.

OTHELLO: Not at all, not at all.

IAGO: Honestly, I am afraid it has. I hope you will remember that the things I have said come from my love for you. But I see that your feelings are hurt, so please do not talk about any larger or more monstrous issues than these suspicions.

OTHELLO: I will not.

IAGO: If you did, my lord, I would say terrible things that I would regret. Cassio is my worthy friend—My lord, I see you are sad.

OTHELLO: No, not really sad. I believe Desdemona is honest.

IAGO: May she have a long, honest life and may you continue trusting her for a long time!

OTHELLO: And yet, how nature makes mistakes—

IAGO: Yes, also there is the point that—if I may speak openly with you– she had turned down the many offers of marriage from people from her own country, color, and social position: you would think, that this is the natural course of things. Pew! One can smell a rotting, disgusting imbalance that goes against nature. But excuse me. I am not talking specifically about

Foul disproportion, thoughts unnatural.
But pardon me. I do not in position
Distinctly speak of her; though I may fear,
265   Her will, recoiling to her better judgement,
May fall to match you with her country forms,
And happily repent.

OTHELLO: Farewell, farewell:
If more thou dost perceive, let me know more;
270   Set on thy wife to observe. Leave me, Iago.

IAGO: *[Going.]* My lord, I take my leave.

OTHELLO: Why did I marry? This honest creature doubtless
Sees and knows more, much more, than he unfolds.

IAGO: *[Returning.]* My lord, I would I might entreat your honor
275   To scan this thing no further; leave it to time:
Though it be fit that Cassio have his place,
For sure he fills it up with great ability,
Yet, if you please to hold him off awhile,
You shall by that perceive him and his means:
280   Note if your lady strain his entertainment
With any strong or vehement importunity;
Much will be seen in that. In the meantime,
Let me be thought too busy in my fears—
As worthy cause I have to fear I am—
285   And hold her free, I do beseech your honor.

OTHELLO: Fear not my government.

IAGO: I once more take my leave.   *[Exit.]*

OTHELLO: This fellow's of exceeding honesty,
And knows all qualities, with a learned spirit,
290   Of human dealings. If I do prove her haggard,
Though that her jesses were my dear heartstrings,

Desdemona. I am afraid her disposition, rebelling against her better judg-ment, might try to compare you against her own people and regret her deci-sion to have married.

OTHELLO: *Farewell, farewell. If you think of anything else, let me know. Get your wife to watch Desdemona. Let me be, Iago.*

IAGO: [Going] *My lord, I take my leave.*

OTHELLO: *Why did I get married? This honest creature no doubt sees and knows more, much more, than he reveals.*

IAGO: [Returning] *My lord, I wonder if I could get you to stop thinking about this and just give it time to work out. Even though it is appropriate that Cassio have his position—because he definitely has the ability, perhaps if you wait to reinstate him, you will learn more about him and his intentions. Take note if your lady, with strong persistence, insists that you entertain and listen to him. A great deal will be revealed by that. In the meantime, you should think that I am too preoccupied by my own fears—which I believe I am—and regard her as innocent; I do beg your honor.*

OTHELLO: *Do not fear my self control.*

IAGO: *I will leave you once more.* [Exit]

OTHELLO: *This fellow is extremely honest, and is educated in all the qualities of human behavior. If I do prove that she is a wild hawk, even though her leashes are the strings attached to my heart, I will let her go and allow her to survive on her own and live as she wishes. Perhaps, because I am black*

I'ld whistle her off and let her down the wind
To prey at fortune. Haply, for I am black
And have not those soft parts of conversation
295   That chamberers have, or for I am declined
Into the vale of years—yet that's not much—
She's gone. I am abused, and my relief
Must be to loathe her. O curse of marriage,
That we can call these delicate creatures ours,
300   And not their appetites! I had rather be a toad,
And live upon the vapor of a dungeon,
Than keep a corner in the thing I love
For others' uses. Yet, 'tis the plague of great ones;
Prerogatived are they less than the base;
305   'Tis destiny unshunnable, like death:
Even then this forked plague is fated to us
When we do quicken. Desdemona comes:

[Reenter Desdemona and Emilia.]
If she be false, O, then heaven mocks itself!
I'll not believe't.

310   DESD: How now, my dear Othello!
Your dinner, and the generous islanders
By you invited, do attend your presence.

OTHELLO: I am to blame.

DESD: Why do you speak so faintly?
315   Are you not well?

OTHELLO: I have a pain upon my forehead here.

DESD: Faith, that's with watching; 'twill away again:
Let me but bind it hard, within this hour
It will be well.

134

and do not have the eloquence to speak like a gentleman and because I am older—there aren't many other reasons—she's gone. I have been wronged, and my relief will be to despise her. Oh, the curse of marriage is that we can call these delicate creatures ours, but not their desires! I would rather be a toad and live on the foul gases of a dungeon, than to have only a part of what I love and allow the rest to be used by others. But, that is the plague of great ones. They have fewer choices than the common people. It is an unavoidable destiny, like death. Being a victim of adultery is given to many men when we are born. Here comes Desdemona.

[Reenter Desdemona and Emilia]
If she is unfaithful, then heaven mocks itself! I will not believe it.

DESD: *Greetings, my dear Othello! Your dinner and the generous islanders who you invited are waiting for you.*

OTHELLO: *It is my fault.*

DESD: *Why do you speak so quietly? Are you sick?*

OTHELLO: *I have a headache.*

DESD: *By my faith, it's from too much work; it will go away soon. Let me bandage it well, and within an hour, it will subside.*

320 OTHELLO: Your napkin is too little;

> *[He puts the handkerchief from him, and she drops it.]*

Let it alone. Come, I'll go in with you.

DESD: I am very sorry that you are not well.

> *[Exeunt Othello and Desdemona]*

EMILIA: I am glad I have found this napkin:
This was her first remembrance from the Moor:
325 My wayward husband hath a hundred times
Woo'd me to steal it; but she so loves the token,
For he conjured her she should ever keep it,
That she reserves it evermore about her
To kiss and talk to. I'll have the work ta'en out,
330 And give't Iago. What he will do with it
Heaven knows, not I;
I nothing but to please his fantasy.

[Reenter Iago]

IAGO: How now, what do you here alone?

EMILIA: Do not you chide; I have a thing for you.

335 IAGO: A thing for me? It is a common thing—

EMILIA: Ha!

IAGO: To have a foolish wife.

EMILIA: O, is that all? What will you give me now
For that same handkerchief?

340 IAGO: What handkerchief?

EMILIA: What handkerchief?
Why, that the Moor first gave to Desdemona;
That which so often you did bid me steal.

136

OTHELLO: *Your napkin is too small:* [He pushes the handkerchief away from his head, and Desdemona drops it on the floor] *Leave it alone. Come, I'll go in with you.*

DESD: *I am very sorry that you are not well.*

[Exit Othello and Desdemona]

EMILIA: *I am glad I have found this handkerchief. This was Desdemona's first gift from Othello. My unreasonable husband has tried to get me to steal it a hundred times, but she loves the token so much. He told her that she should always keep it, so she always has it with her to kiss and talk to. I'll have the embroidery copied and give the duplicate to Iago; only heaven knows what he intends to do with it. I want only to please his whim.*

[Reenter Iago]

IAGO: *Greetings! What are you doing here alone?*

EMILIA: *Don't scold me. I have something for you.*

IAGO: *Something for me? It is something ordinary—*

EMILIA: *Ha!*

IAGO: *What a foolish wife.*

EMILIA: *Oh, is that all? What will you give me for the same handkerchief?*

IAGO: *What handkerchief?*

EMILIA: *What handkerchief? Why, the first gift from the Moor to Desdemona, the one you have asked me to steal so often.*

IAGO: Hast stol'n it from her?

345 EMILIA: No, faith; she let it drop by negligence,
     And, to the advantage, I being here took't up.
     Look, here it is.

IAGO: A good wench; give it me.

EMILIA: What will you do with't, that you have been so earnest
350   To have me filch it?

IAGO: *[Snatching it.]* Why, what is that to you?

EMILIA: If't be not for some purpose of import,
     Give't me again. Poor lady, she'll run mad
     When she shall lack it.

355 IAGO: Be not acknown on't; I have use for it.
     Go, leave me.   *[Exit Emilia.]*
     I will in Cassio's lodging lose this napkin,
     And let him find it. Trifles light as air
     Are to the jealous confirmations strong
360   As proofs of holy writ; this may do something.
     The Moor already changes with my poison:
     Dangerous conceits are in their natures poisons,
     Which at the first are scarce found to distaste,
     But with a little act upon the blood
365   Burn like the mines of sulphur. I did say so:
     Look, where he comes!

     [Reenter Othello]
     Not poppy, nor mandragora,
     Nor all the drowsy syrups of the world,
     Shall ever medicine thee to that sweet sleep
370   Which thou owedst yesterday.

OTHELLO: Ha, ha, false to me?

138

IAGO: Have you stolen it from her?

EMILIA: No. She dropped it by accident, and, luckily, I, being here, picked it up. Look, here it is.

IAGO: What a good girl. Give it to me.

EMILIA: What will you do with it; why were you so eager to have me steal it?

IAGO: [Snatching it] Why does that matter to you?

EMILIA: If it is not for some important purpose, give it back to me. The poor lady will go mad when she realizes it is missing.

IAGO: Don't say anything about this. I have a use for it. Go, leave me.

[Exit Emilia]

I will place this handkerchief in Cassio's apartment and let him find it. Small items, as light as air, will confirm what jealous people believe and give them proof that is as unquestionable as the words of Holy Scripture. The Moor has already changed since I poisoned his thoughts with suspicions. Ideas are as dangerous as poison in their own way because at first they seem only a little sour, but when they begin to work in the blood, they burn like sulfur mines. Look, here he comes!

[Reenter Othello]

No sleep-inducing plants like poppies or mandrake, nor all the sleeping potions in the world, will ever give you, Othello, the sweet, deep sleep that you had yesterday.

OTHELLO: Ha! ha! Lying to me?

139

IAGO: Why, how now, general! No more of that.

OTHELLO: Avaunt! be gone! Thou hast set me on the rack:
I swear 'tis better to be much abused
375   Than but to know't a little.

IAGO: How now, my lord?

OTHELLO: What sense had I of her stol'n hours of lust?
I saw't not, thought it not, it harm'd not me;
I slept the next night well, was free and merry;
380   I found not Cassio's kisses on her lips:
He that is robb'd, not wanting what is stol'n,
Let him not know't and he's not robb'd at all.

IAGO: I am sorry to hear this.

OTHELLO: I had been happy if the general camp,
385   Pioners and all, had tasted her sweet body,
So I had nothing known. O, now forever
Farewell the tranquil mind! Farewell content!
Farewell the plumed troop and the big wars
That make ambition virtue! O, farewell,
390   Farewell the neighing steed and the shrill trump,
The spiritstirring drum, the earpiercing fife,
The royal banner, and all quality,
Pride, pomp, and circumstance of glorious war!
And O you mortal engines, whose rude throats
395   The immortal Jove's dread clamors counterfeit,
Farewell! Othello's occupation's gone!

IAGO: Is't possible, my lord?

OTHELLO: Villain, be sure thou prove my love a whore;
Be sure of it. Give me the ocular proof;
400   Or, by the worth of man's eternal soul,
Thou hadst been better have been born a dog
Than answer my waked wrath!

140

IAGO: *Why, hello, general! No more of that kind of talk.*

OTHELLO: *Go! Be gone! You have put me on the torturing rack. I swear it is bet-ter to be deceived than it is to know even a little.*

IAGO: *What do you mean, my lord?*

OTHELLO: *What did I know about her secret hours of lust? I didn't see it, didn't think about it, and it did not hurt me. I slept well last night, was free and happy. I did not find Cassio's kisses on her lips. A person may be robbed, but if he has no knowledge of what has been stolen, ultimately, he has not been robbed at all.*

IAGO: *I am sorry to hear this.*

OTHELLO: *I would have been happier if every soldier in camp had tasted her sweet body, and I had known nothing about it. Oh, now, good-bye forever to the peaceful mind! Good-bye contentment! Farewell to the decorated troops and the big wars that make ambition an asset! Oh, farewell! Farewell the neighing horse, the screeching trumpet, the spirit-stirring drum, the ear-piercing flute, the royal banner, and all quality, pride, magnificence, and customs of glorious war! And, oh, you cannons, whose rude throats mimic the immortal Jove's thunder, farewell! Othello's occupation is gone!*

IAGO: *Is it possible, my lord?*

OTHELLO: *Villain, be sure you can prove that my love is a whore.* [Grabbing Othello by the throat.] *Be sure of it. Give me proof I can see, or by the worth of man's eternal soul, you will wish that you were born a dog rather than to be forced to answer to my awakened rage!*

IAGO: Is't come to this?

OTHELLO: Make me to see't; or at the least so prove it,
405   That the probation bear no hinge nor loop
     To hang a doubt on; or woe upon thy life!

IAGO: My noble lord

OTHELLO: If thou dost slander her and torture me,
     Never pray more; abandon all remorse;
410   On horror's head horrors accumulate.
     Do deeds to make heaven weep, all earth amazed;
     For nothing canst thou to damnation add
     Greater than that.

IAGO: O grace! O heaven defend me!
415   Are you a man? have you a soul or sense?
     God be wi' you; take mine office. O wretched fool,
     That livest to make thine honesty a vice!
     O monstrous world! Take note, take note, O world,
     To be direct and honest is not safe.
420   I thank you for this profit, and from hence
     I'll love no friend sith love breeds such offense.

OTHELLO: Nay, stay; thou shouldst be honest.

IAGO: I should be wise; for honesty's a fool,
     And loses that it works for.

425 OTHELLO: By the world,
       I think my wife be honest, and think she is not;
       I think that thou art just, and think thou art not.
       I'll have some proof. Her name, that was as fresh
       As Dian's visage, is now begrimed and black
430   As mine own face. If there be cords or knives,
       Poison or fire, or suffocating streams,
       I'll not endure it. Would I were satisfied!

IAGO: Has it come to this?

OTHELLO: Make me see it, or at least prove it. Prove that your investigation leaves no tiny room for doubt, or your life will be miserable!

IAGO: My noble lord—

OTHELLO: If you lie about her and torture me, prayer will not help you, so abandon your conscience. On horror's head more horrors will gather. You may do deeds that make the heavens weep and confuse the world. There is nothing you can do, however, to add to your damnation that will be greater than this.

IAGO: Oh, grace! Oh, heaven defend me! Are you a man? Have you a soul or sense? God be with you; take away my position. Oh, what a miserable fool I am that I should live to make my honesty a weakness! Oh, monstrous world! Take note, take note, oh, world; to be direct and honest is not safe. I thank you for this lesson, and from now on I will not love a friend, since love leads to such an accusation.

OTHELLO: No, stay. You need to be honest.

IAGO: I should be wise; being honest is foolish because it ends up losing what it is working for.

OTHELLO: For the entire world, I think my wife is honest and yet think she is not. I think that you are just and yet think you are not. I need some proof. Her name, which was as fresh as a vision of Diana, is now dirty and black as my own face. If cords or knives, poison or fire, or suffocating streams were available, I wouldn't endure this. I must be satisfied!

IAGO: I see, sir, you are eaten up with passion;
I do repent me that I put it to you.
435 You would be satisfied?

OTHELLO: Would? Nay, I will.

IAGO: And may. But, how? how satisfied, my lord?
Would you, the supervisor, grossly gape on?
Behold her topp'd?

440 OTHELLO: Death and damnation! O!

IAGO: It were a tedious difficulty, I think,
To bring them to that prospect. Damn them then,
If ever mortal eyes do see them bolster
More than their own! What then? how then?
445 What shall I say? Where's satisfaction?
It is impossible you should see this
Were they as prime as goats, as hot as monkeys,
As salt as wolves in pride, and fools as gross
As ignorance made drunk. But yet, I say,
If imputation and strong circumstances,
450 Which lead directly to the door of truth,
Will give you satisfaction, you may have't.

OTHELLO: Give me a living reason she's disloyal.

IAGO: I do not like the office;
But sith I am enter'd in this cause so far,
Prick'd to't by foolish honesty and love,
455 I will go on. I lay with Cassio lately
And, being troubled with a raging tooth,
I could not sleep.
There are a kind of men so loose of soul,
That in their sleeps will mutter their affairs;
460 One of this kind is Cassio
In sleep I heard him say, "Sweet Desdemona,

144

IAGO: I see, sir, that you are consumed with passion.
I am sorry that I ever spoke of this. How would you be satisfied?

OTHELLO: Would be? No, I will be.

IAGO: Yes, but, how? What would satisfy you my lord? Would you like some
kind of spectator to stare disgustedly at them in the act?

OTHELLO: Death and damnation! Oh!

IAGO: It would be extremely difficult, I think, to bring that into view. Damn
them; only if mortal eyes, other than their own, see them committing adultery. What then? How then? What should I say? How will you be satisfied?
It is impossible for you to see this, even if they were as eager as goats, as hot
as monkeys, as lustful as wolves in pride, and as foolish as drunken idiots.
But, I say, if rumors and strong circumstantial evidence that leads directly
to the truth, will give you satisfaction, you may have it.

OTHELLO: Give me a real example of her disloyalty.

IAGO: I do not like this job. But, since I am involved this much, pushed forward
by foolish honesty and love, I will go on. I have slept next to Cassio lately,
and, being bothered with a toothache, I could not sleep. Some men, whose
souls are so relaxed, mumble the secrets they keep while they sleep. Cassio
is like that. In his sleep I heard him say, "Sweet Desdemona, let's be careful,
we have to hide our love." Then, sir, he gripped and squeezed my hand and
cried, "Oh, sweet creature!" and then he kissed me hard, as if kisses grew on
my lips and he were picking them by the roots. Then he laid his leg over my
thigh, and sighed, and kissed; then he cried, "What a tragic fate that you are
married to the Moor!"

Let us be wary, let us hide our loves";
And then, sir, would he gripe and wring my hand,
Cry, "O sweet creature!" and then kiss me hard,
465 As if he pluck'd up kisses by the roots,
That grew upon my lips; then laid his leg
Over my thigh, and sigh'd and kiss'd; and then
Cried, "Cursed fate that gave thee to the Moor!"

OTHELLO: O monstrous! monstrous!

470 IAGO: Nay, this was but his dream.

OTHELLO: But this denoted a foregone conclusion:
'Tis a shrewd doubt, though it be but a dream.

IAGO: And this may help to thicken other proofs
That do demonstrate thinly.

475 OTHELLO: I'll tear her all to pieces.

IAGO: Nay, but be wise; yet we see nothing done;
She may be honest yet. Tell me but this;
Have you not sometimes seen a handkerchief
Spotted with strawberries in your wife's hand?

480 OTHELLO: I gave her such a one; 'twas my first gift.

IAGO: I know not that; but such a handkerchief—
I am sure it was your wife's—did I today
See Cassio wipe his beard with.

OTHELLO: If it be that—

485 IAGO: If it be that, or any that was hers,
It speaks against her with the other proofs.

OTHELLO: O, that the slave had forty thousand lives!

146

OTHELLO: *Oh, monstrous, monstrous!*

IAGO: *No, remember this was only his dream.*

OTHELLO: *But, it represents previous occurrence. Even though it is only a dream, it raises questions.*

IAGO: *And this may help to reinforce other evidence, which is not enough by itself.*

OTHELLO: *I'll tear her to pieces.*

IAGO: *No, be wise. We still have not seen anything done. She may still be honorable. Tell me this: Have you ever seen your wife holding a handkerchief embroidered with strawberries?*

OTHELLO: *I gave her a handkerchief like that. It was my first gift.*

IAGO: *I didn't know that, but a handkerchief like that—I am sure it was your wife's—I saw Cassio wipe his beard with today.*

OTHELLO: *If it was that one—*

IAGO: *If it was that handkerchief or any of hers, it is proof, along with everything else.*

OTHELLO: *Oh, I wish that the slave had forty thousand lives! One lifetime is not*

One is too poor, too weak for my revenge.
Now do I see 'tis true. Look here, Iago;
490 All my fond love thus do I blow to heaven:
'Tis gone.
Arise, black vengeance, from thy hollow cell!
Yield up, O love, thy crown and hearted throne
To tyrannous hate! Swell, bosom, with thy fraught,
495 For 'tis of aspics' tongues!

IAGO: Yet be content.

OTHELLO: O, blood, blood, blood!

IAGO: Patience, I say; your mind perhaps may change.

OTHELLO: Never, Iago: Like to the Pontic Sea,
500 Whose icy current and compulsive course
Ne'er feels retiring ebb, but keeps due on
To the Propontic and the Hellespont,
Even so my bloody thoughts, with violent pace,
Shall ne'er look back, ne'er ebb to humble love,
505 Till that a capable and wide revenge
Swallow them up. Now, by yond marble heaven,
In the due reverence of a sacred vow
[Kneels.] I here engage my words.

IAGO: Do not rise yet.
510 [Kneels.] Witness, you everburning lights above,
You elements that clip us round about,
Witness that here Iago doth give up
The execution of his wit, hands, heart,
To wrong'd Othello's service! Let him command,
515 And to obey shall be in me remorse,
What bloody business ever.   [They rise.]

OTHELLO: I greet thy love,
Not with vain thanks, but with acceptance bounteous, And will
upon the instant put thee to't:

148

enough for me to get revenge. Now I see it is true. Look here, Iago, all my love for Cassio I now throw up to heaven. It is gone. My dark revenge, rise up from your hollow cell! Oh, love, give up your crown and precious throne for cruel hatred! May my heart swell with this burden made from the tongues of poisonous snakes.

IAGO: *Now calm down.*

OTHELLO: *Oh, blood, blood, blood!*

IAGO: *Have patience, I say; perhaps you will change your mind.*

OTHELLO: *Never, Iago. I am like the Black Sea, whose icy and forward current never has a retreating tide but keeps heading toward its destination and toward the Hellespont. My bloody thoughts, also rushing at a violent pace, will never look back, will never retreat to kind love until a suitable and all-encompassing revenge swallows Cassio and Desdemona up. Now, by far-off heaven, paying the highest respect to a sacred promise,* [Kneels] *I pledge my word.*

IAGO: *Do not get up yet.* [Kneels] *You perpetual lights above, the wind and air that circle around us, witness and testify to the fact that Iago gives up the use of his will, his hands, his heart, to the betrayed Othello! Let Othello command, and I will obey and do whatever bloody business he asks.*

OTHELLO: *I welcome your love, not with worthless thanks, but with openhearted approval, and I will give you a job this very instant. Within three days let me hear you say that Cassio is dead.*

520   Within these three days let me hear thee say
       That Cassio's not alive.

IAGO: My friend is dead, 'tis done at your request;
       But let her live.

OTHELLO: Damn her, lewd minx! O, damn her!
525   Come, go with me apart; I will withdraw,
       To furnish me with some swift means of death
       For the fair devil. Now art thou my lieutenant.

IAGO: I am your own forever.

[Exeunt.]

SCENE 4
Before the castle.

[Enter Desdemona, Emilia, and Clown.]

DESD: Do you know, sirrah, where Lieutenant Cassio lies?

CLOWN. I dare not say he lies anywhere.

DESD: Why, man?

CLOWN. He's a soldier; and for one to say a soldier lies, is stabbing.

5   DESD: Go to! Where lodges he?

CLOWN. To tell you where he lodges, is to tell you where I lie.

DESD: Can anything be made of this?

CLOWN. I know not where he lodges, and for me to devise a lodging,
       and say he lies here or he lies there, were to lie in mine own throat.

IAGO: *My friend is dead. It is done at your request; but let Desdemona live.*

OTHELLO: *Damn her, lustful, wild woman! Oh, damn her! Come with me; I will leave, to think of some swift means of death for the beautiful devil. Now you are my lieutenant.*

IAGO: *I am your loyal servant forever.*

[Exeunt]

SCENE IV
In front of the castle.

[Enter Desdemona, Emilia, and Clown]

DESD: *Do you know, sir, where Lieutenant Cassio lies?*

CLOWN: *I cannot say that he lies anywhere.*

DESD: *What, man?*

CLOWN: *He is a soldier, and to say a soldier lies is stabbing him.*

DESD: *All right. Where is he staying?*

CLOWN: *To tell you where he is staying, is to tell you where I lie.*

DESD: *Can anything be made of this nonsense?*

CLOWN: *I do not know where he stays, and for me to invent a place and say he lies here or he lies there would be my own lie.*

10 DESD: Can you inquire him out and be edified by report?

CLOWN. I will catechize the world for him; that is, make questions and by them answer.

DESD: Seek him, bid him come hither. Tell him I have moved my lord on his behalf and hope all will be well.

15 CLOWN. To do this is within the compass of man's wit, and therefore I will attempt the doing it.   [Exit.]

DESD: Where should I lose that handkerchief, Emilia?

EMILIA: I know not, madam.

DESD: Believe me, I had rather have lost my purse
20   Full of crusadoes; and, but my noble Moor
        Is true of mind and made of no such baseness
        As jealous creatures are, it were enough
        To put him to ill thinking.

EMILIA: Is he not jealous?

25 DESD: Who, he? I think the sun where he was born
        Drew all such humors from him.

EMILIA: Look, where he comes.

DESD: I will not leave him now till Cassio
        Be call'd to him.

[Enter Othello.]
30   How is't with you, my lord?

OTHELLO: Well, my good lady. [Aside.] O, hardness to dissemble!
        How do you, Desdemona?

DESD: Can you find out where he is and inform me?

CLOWN: I will quiz the world for him. That is, I will make up questions and find answers.

DESD: Look for him, and ask him to come here. Tell him I have convinced my lord on his behalf, and I hope all will be well.

CLOWN: To do this is within the range of man's abilities, and, therefore, I will attempt to do it.   [Exit]

DESD: Where did I lose that handkerchief, Emilia?

EMILIA: I don't know, madam.

DESD: Believe me, I would rather have lost my purse full of gold coins. But my noble Moor has a clear mind and does not have the kind of meanness that jealous people have. If he were, this would be enough to make him think the worst.

EMILIA: He is not jealous?

DESD: Who, Othello? I think the sunny climate where he was born drew all such ill-temper out of him.

EMILIA: Look, here he comes.

DESD: I will stay with Othello now until he calls Cassio here.

[Enter Othello]
     How are you, my lord?

OTHELLO: I am well, my good lady.
          [Aside] Oh, it is difficult to lie! How are you, Desdemona?

DESD: Well, my good lord.

OTHELLO: Give me your hand. This hand is moist, my lady.

35 DESD: It yet has felt no age nor known no sorrow:

OTHELLO: This argues fruitfulness and liberal heart;
    Hot, hot, and moist. This hand of yours requires
    A sequester from liberty, fasting and prayer,
    Much castigation, exercise devout,
40   For here's a young and sweating devil here
    That commonly rebels. 'Tis a good hand,
    A frank one.

DESD: You may, indeed, say so;
    For 'twas that hand that gave away my heart.

45 OTHELLO: A liberal hand. The hearts of old gave hands;
    But our new heraldry is hands, not hearts.

DESD: I cannot speak of this. Come now, your promise.

OTHELLO: What promise, chuck?

DESD: I have sent to bid Cassio come speak with you.

50 OTHELLO: I have a salt and sorry rheum offends me;
    Lend me thy handkerchief.

DESD: Here, my lord.

OTHELLO: That which I gave you.

DESD: I have it not about me.

55 OTHELLO: Not?

DESD: Well, my good lord.

OTHELLO: Give me your hand. This hand is damp, my lady.

DESD: It has not felt age or sorrow yet.

OTHELLO: This damp hand indicates generosity and a kind heart. Hot, hot, and moist. This hand of yours requires a separation from liberty, fasting and prayer, a lot of purification, and devout prayers. Yes, this hand is a young and sweating devil that usually rebels. It is a good hand, a honest hand.

DESD: You may accurately say so, because it was that hand that gave my heart away.

OTHELLO: A generous hand. At one time, people used to marry out of love, but now, marriage has become a formality, a kind of shallow ceremony, where hands are given away, not hearts.

DESD: I cannot speak about this. Come now; remember your promise.

OTHELLO: What promise, my dear?

DESD: I have sent for Cassio to come and speak with you.

OTHELLO: I am teary, and an awful cold bothers me. Lend me your handkerchief.

DESD: Here, my lord.

OTHELLO: The one which I gave you.

DESD: I do not have it with me

OTHELLO: No?

DESD: No, faith, my lord.

OTHELLO: That's a fault. That handkerchief
Did an Egyptian to my mother give;
She was a charmer, and could almost read
60   The thoughts of people. She told her, while she kept it,
'Twould make her amiable and subdue my father
Entirely to her love, but if she lost it
Or made a gift of it, my father's eye
Should hold her loathed and his spirits should hunt
65   After new fancies. She dying gave it me,
And bid me, when my fate would have me wive,
To give it her. I did so, and take heed on't;
Make it a darling like your precious eye;
To lose't or give't away were such perdition
70   As nothing else could match.

DESD: Is't possible?

OTHELLO: 'Tis true; there's magic in the web of it.
A sibyl, that had number'd in the world
The sun to course two hundred compasses,
75   In her prophetic fury sew'd the work;
The worms were hallow'd that did breed the silk,
And it was dyed in mummy which the skillful
Conserved of maidens' hearts.

DESD: Indeed! is't true?

80   OTHELLO: Most veritable; therefore look to't well.

DESD: Then would to God that I had never seen't!

OTHELLO: Ha! wherefore?

DESD: Why do you speak so startingly and rash?

156

DESD: *No, indeed, my lord.*

OTHELLO: *That is a mistake. An Egyptian gave that handkerchief to my mother. She was a psychic and could almost read people's thoughts. She told my mother that the handkerchief would make her sweet, and my father would be completely controlled by her love. But if she lost it or gave it away, my father would see only hatred for her, and he would hunt after new lovers. My mother gave it to me on her deathbed and told me that when it was time for me to marry, I should give it to my wife. I did so; and seriously consider this, make it as cherished as your precious eyesight. To lose it or give it away would cause such disaster that nothing else could match it.*

DESD: *Is this possible?*

OTHELLO: *It is true. There is magic in the knitting of it. A fortune-teller who lived for two hundred years sewed the handkerchief in a prophetic fury. Holy worms spun the silk, and it was dyed in a fluid made from skillfully preserved maidens' hearts.*

DESD: *Honestly! Is this true?*

OTHELLO: *Absolutely true. Therefore, take good care of it.*

DESD: *Then I wish to God that I had never seen it!*

OTHELLO: *Ha! Why?*

DESD: *Why are you speaking so frighteningly and recklessly?*

OTHELLO: Is't lost? is't gone? speak, is it out o' the way?

85 DESD: Heaven bless us!

OTHELLO: Say you?

DESD: It is not lost; but what an if it were?

OTHELLO: How?

DESD: I say, it is not lost.

90 OTHELLO: Fetch't, let me see it.

DESD: Why, so I can, sir, but I will not now.
       This is a trick to put me from my suit.
       Pray you, let Cassio be received again.

OTHELLO: Fetch me the handkerchief, my mind misgives.

95 DESD: Come, come; You'll never meet a more sufficient man.

OTHELLO: The handkerchief!

DESD: I pray, talk me of Cassio:

OTHELLO: The handkerchief!

DESD: A man that all his time
100   Hath founded his good fortunes on your love,
       Shared dangers with you—

OTHELLO: The handkerchief!

DESD: In sooth, you are to blame.

OTHELLO: Away!   [Exit.]

158

OTHELLO: *Is it lost? Is it gone? Speak up; is it put away?*

DESD: *Heaven bless us!*

OTHELLO: *What do you say?*

DESD: *It is not lost, but what if it were?*

OTHELLO: *How?*

DESD: *I say, it is not lost.*

OTHELLO: *Get it, let me see it.*

DESD: *Well, I can get it, sir, but not now. This is a trick to distract me from my cause. I beg you, let Cassio speak to you.*

OTHELLO: *Get me the handkerchief. My mind tells me that evil is present.*

DESD: *Come, come. You will never meet a better man than Cassio.*

OTHELLO: *The handkerchief!*

DESD: *I beg you, talk to me about Cassio.*

OTHELLO: *The handkerchief!*

DESD: *A man that, at all times, has based his good fortunes on your love, shared dangers with you—*

OTHELLO: *The handkerchief!*

DESD: *In truth, you are to blame.*

OTHELLO: *I'm leaving!*   [Exit]

105   Emilia: Is not this man jealous?

Desd: I ne'er saw this before.
     Sure there's some wonder in this handkerchief;
     I am most unhappy in the loss of it.

Emilia: 'Tis not a year or two shows us a man:
110   They are all but stomachs and we all but food;
     They eat us hungerly, and when they are full
     They belch us. Look you! Cassio and my husband.

[Enter Cassio and Iago.]

Iago: There is no other way; 'tis she must do't:
     And, lo, the happiness! Go and importune her.

115   Desd: How now, good Cassio! What's the news with you?

Cassio: Madam, my former suit: I do beseech you
     That by your virtuous means I may again
     Exist and be a member of his love
     Whom I with all the office of my heart
120   Entirely honor. I would not be delay'd.
     If my offense be of such mortal kind
     That nor my service past nor present sorrows
     Nor purposed merit in futurity
     Can ransom me into his love again,
125   But to know so must be my benefit;
     So shall I clothe me in a forced content
     And shut myself up in some other course
     To Fortune's alms.

Desd: Alas, thrice gentle Cassio!
130   My advocation is not now in tune;
     My lord is not my lord, nor should I know him
     Were he in favor as in humor alter'd.
     So help me every spirit sanctified,

EMILIA: *Doesn't this man seem jealous?*

DESD: *I never saw him like this before. Certainly, there's some magic in this handkerchief. I am very unhappy about losing it.*

EMILIA: *You cannot get to know a man in a year or two. They are all stomachs, and we are merely their food, which they eat hungrily, and when they are full, they belch us up. Look there, Cassio and my husband.*

[Enter Cassio and Iago]

IAGO: *There is no other way. It is Desdemona who must do it. And, look, what luck! Go, and ask her.*

DESD: *Greetings, good Cassio! What is the news with you?*

CASSIO: *Madam, it's my previous request: I beg you to let your goodness work on my behalf so that I can return to work for the man I love, because I, with all the good will in my heart, truly honor Othello. Do not delay. If my crime is so bad that my past service, present sorrow, or future usefulness can not save me, it will benefit me to know this soon. I will force myself to be content and will resign myself and find another occupation.*

DESD: *Alas, gentle Cassio! It is not a good time for me to defend you. My lord is not himself, and I don't know him right now; if he were in a better mood, perhaps. Believe me, I have spoken well of you, even though he did not like it. You must be patient for a time. I will do what I can. And I will dare more for you than I would for myself. Let that be enough for you.*

As I have spoken for you all my best

135   And stood within the blank of his displeasure

For my free speech! You must awhile be patient.

What I can do I will; and more I will

Than for myself I dare. Let that suffice you.

IAGO: Is my lord angry?

140 EMILIA: He went hence but now,

And certainly in strange unquietness.

IAGO: Can he be angry? I have seen the cannon,

When it hath blown his ranks into the air

And, like the devil, from his very arm

145   Puff'd his own brother. And can he be angry?

Something of moment then. I will go meet him:

There's matter in't indeed if he be angry.

DESD: I prithee, do so.   *[Exit Iago.]*

Something sure of state,

150   Either from Venice or some unhatch'd practice

Made demonstrable here in Cyprus to him,

Hath puddled his clear spirit; and in such cases

Men's natures wrangle with inferior things,

Though great ones are their object. 'Tis even so;

155   For let our finger ache, and it indues

Our other healthful members even to that sense

Of pain. Nay, we must think men are not gods,

I was, unhandsome warrior as I am,

Arraigning his unkindness with my soul;

160   But now I find I had suborn'd the witness,

And he's indicted falsely.

EMILIA: Pray heaven it be state matters, as you think,

And no conception nor no jealous toy

Concerning you.

IAGO: *Is my lord angry?*

EMILIA: *He went away just now, and he was certainly in strange mood.*

IAGO: *Is he angry? I have seen the cannon, when it has blown his men into the air, and, like the devil, pulled Othello's own brother from his arm. Can he be angry? It is something important then. I will go meet him. If he is angry, there is indeed something wrong.*

DESD: *I beg you, please do so. [Exit Iago] Something concerning official business, either from Venice, or something he discovered here in Cyprus disturbs his good spirits. At such times, people get upset by little things, even though it is great things that are the cause. Even so, if your finger hurts, you start to ache all over. We must remember that men are not gods, nor should we expect them to act like a bride. Emilia, scold me; I was, inadequate soldier that I am, judging his anger with my soul, but now I find that I lied and convicted him falsely.*

EMILIA: *I pray to heaven that it is state matters, as you think, and not jealous thoughts concerning you.*

165 DESD: Alas the day, I never gave him cause!

EMILIA: But jealous souls will not be answer'd so;
    They are not ever jealous for the cause,
    But jealous for they are jealous. 'Tis a monster
    Begot upon itself, born on itself.

170 DESD: Heaven keep that monster from Othello's mind!

EMILIA: Lady, amen.

DESD: I will go seek him. Cassio, walk hereabout.
    If I do find him fit, I'll move your suit,
    And seek to effect it to my uttermost.

175 CASSIO: I humbly thank your ladyship.
                            [Exeunt Desdemona and Emilia.]

[Enter Bianca.]

BIANCA: Save you, friend Cassio!

CASSIO: What make you from home?
    How is it with you, my most fair Bianca?
    I'faith, sweet love, I was coming to your house.

180 BIANCA: And I was going to your lodging, Cassio
    What, keep a week away? seven days and nights?
    Eight score eight hours? and lovers' absent hours,
    More tedious than the dial eight score times?
    O weary reckoning!

185 CASSIO: Pardon me, Bianca:
    I have this while with leaden thoughts been press'd;
    But I shall in a more continuate time
    Strike off this score of absence. Sweet Bianca,
            [Gives her Desdemona's handkerchief.]
    Take me this work out.

DESD: *I rue this day; I never gave him cause to be jealous.*

EMILIA: *But jealous souls are not always jealous for a good cause. They are jealous because they are jealous. Jealousy is a monster produced from itself, born by itself.*

DESD: *Heaven keep that monster from Othello's mind!*

EMILIA: *Lady, Amen.*

DESD: *I will go look for him. Cassio, walk around here. If I find Othello in a good mood, I'll advance your case and try my best to help you.*

CASSIO: *I humbly thank your ladyship.*

[Exit Desdemona and Emilia]

[Enter Bianca]

BIANCA: *Good day, friend Cassio!*

CASSIO: *What brings you out of the house? How are you, my most beautiful Bianca? To be honest, love, I was just coming over to your house.*

BIANCA: *And I was going to your house. Cassio, why have you not been around for a week? Seven days and nights? Eight score and eight hours? A lover's hours away from her love are more exhausting than the normal hours are. Oh, these are sad calculations!*

CASSIO: *Forgive me, Bianca; I have had a lot on my mind lately. But I will, in a more undisturbed time, make up for the twenty absences. Sweet Bianca,* [Giving her Desdemona's handkerchief] *copy this pattern.*

165

190 BIANCA: O Cassio, whence came this?
This is some token from a newer friend.
To the felt absence now I feel a cause:
Is't come to this? Well, well.

CASSIO: Go to, woman!
195 Throw your vile guesses in the devil's teeth,
From whence you have them. You are jealous now
That this is from some mistress, some remembrance:
No, by my faith, Bianca.

BIANCA: Why, whose is it?

200 CASSIO: I know not, sweet. I found it in my chamber.
I like the work well. Ere it be demanded—
As like enough it will—I'ld have it copied:
Take it, and do't; and leave me for this time.

BIANCA: Leave you! wherefore?

205 CASSIO: I do attend here on the general;
And think it no addition, nor my wish,
To have him see me woman'd.

BIANCA: Why, I pray you?

CASSIO: Not that I love you not.

210 BIANCA: But that you do not love me.
I pray you, bring me on the way a little;
And say if I shall see you soon at night.

CASSIO: 'Tis but a little way that I can bring you;
For I attend here, but I'll see you soon.

215 BIANCA: 'Tis very good; I must be circumstanced.

[Exeunt.]

BIANCA: Oh, Cassio, where did this come from? This is some token from a newer friend. Now I realize why you were missing. Has it come to this? Well, well.

CASSIO: Get out of here, woman! Throw your despicable guesses into the devil's teeth, back where they came from. You are jealous now because you think this handkerchief is some remembrance from some mistress. No, honestly, Bianca.

BIANCA: Why, whose is it?

CASSIO: I don't know, sweetheart. I found it in my apartment. I like the embroidery. Before it is claimed—as I am sure it will be—I would like to have it copied. Take it, and do it; and leave me for now.

BIANCA: Leave you! Why?

CASSIO: I am waiting here for the general; and it will not help me, nor do I not want him to see me here with a woman.

BIANCA: Why, may I ask?

CASSIO: Not that I don't love you.

BIANCA: But that you do love me not. I beg you, humor me and say that I will see you early tonight.

CASSIO: I can only humor you a little, because now I have to wait here. But I'll see you soon.

BIANCA: That's good; I must accept these circumstances.

[Exeunt]

ACT IV

SCENE 1
Cyprus. Before the castle.

[Enter Othello and Iago]

IAGO: Will you think so?

OTHELLO: Think so, Iago?

IAGO: What, To kiss in private?

OTHELLO: An unauthorized kiss.

5   IAGO: Or to be naked with her friend in bed
     An hour or more, not meaning any harm?

OTHELLO: Naked in bed, Iago, and not mean harm!
     It is hypocrisy against the devil:
     They that mean virtuously and yet do so,
10   The devil their virtue tempts and they tempt heaven.

IAGO: So they do nothing, 'tis a venial slip:
     But if I give my wife a handkerchief

OTHELLO: What then?

IAGO: Why, then, 'tis hers, my lord, and being hers,
15   She may, I think, bestow't on any man.

ACT IV

SCENE I
Cyprus. In front of the castle.

[Enter Othello and Iago]

IAGO: Will you think so?

OTHELLO: Think so, Iago!

IAGO: What, to kiss in private?

OTHELLO: A prohibited kiss.

IAGO: Or to be naked with her friend in bed an hour or more, not meaning any harm?

OTHELLO: Naked in bed, Iago, and not mean harm! It is hypocrisy even to the devil to say you are honest and to do that. The devil tempts the people's goodness through such behavior, and they tempt heaven.

IAGO: So they do nothing, it is a mistake of the flesh.
But if I give my wife a handkerchief—

OTHELLO: What then?

IAGO: Why, then, it is hers, my lord; and, being hers, she may, I think, give it to any man.

OTHELLO: She is protectress of her honor too:
    May she give that?

IAGO: Her honor is an essence that's not seen;
    They have it very oft that have it not:
20   But for the handkerchief—

OTHELLO: By heaven, I would most gladly have forgot it:
    Thou said'st—O, it comes o'er my memory,
    As doth the raven o'er the infected house,
    Boding to all—he had my handkerchief.

25   IAGO: Ay, what of that?

OTHELLO: That's not so good now.

IAGO: What, if I had said I had seen him do you wrong?
    Or heard him say—as knaves be such abroad,
    Who having, by their own importunate suit,
30   Or voluntary dotage of some mistress,
    Convinced or supplied them, cannot choose
    But they must blab—

OTHELLO: Hath he said anything?

IAGO: He hath, my lord; but be you well assured,
35   No more than he'll unswear.

OTHELLO: What hath he said?

IAGO: Faith, that he did—I know not what he did.

OTHELLO: What? what?

IAGO: Lie—

40   OTHELLO: With her?

OTHELLO: *She also is the protector of her honor.*   *Might she give that away?*

IAGO: *Her honor is a quality that's not seen. People often seem to have it who don't have it. But, for the handkerchief—*

OTHELLO: *By heaven, I would gladly have forgotten it. You said it, and it comes over my memory just like a raven flying over an infected house, bringing disease and warning to all.—He had my handkerchief!*

IAGO: *Yes, what of that?*

OTHELLO: *That's not good now.*

IAGO: *What if I had said I had seen Cassio deceive you? Or heard him say that he deceived you—as foreign rogues do when, they seduce a woman through urgent talk or through doting love —and then they must brag about it.*

OTHELLO: *Has he said anything?*

IAGO: *He has, my lord; but you can be sure that he has not said anything that he will not deny.*

OTHELLO: *What has he said?*

IAGO: *Honestly, that he—I don't know exactly what he did.*

OTHELLO: *What? What?*

IAGO: *Lie—*

OTHELLO: *With her?*

IAGO: With her, on her, what you will.

OTHELLO: Lie with her! lie on her!—We say lie on her, when they belie
her.—Lie with her! 'Zounds, that's fulsome! Handkerchief—confessions—handkerchief! To confess and be hanged for his labor
45   first, to be hanged, and then to confess. I tremble at it. Nature
would not invest herself in such shadowing passion without some
instruction. It is not words that shakes me thus. Pish! Noses, ears,
and lips. Is't possible? Confess?—Handkerchief?—O devil!

[Falls in a trance.]

IAGO: Work on,
50   My medicine, work! Thus credulous fools are caught:
And many worthy and chaste dames even thus,
All guiltless, meet reproach. What, ho! My lord!
My lord, I say! Othello!

[Enter Cassio.]
How now, Cassio!

55   CASSIO: What's the matter?

IAGO: My lord is fall'n into an epilepsy:
This is his second fit; he had one yesterday.

CASSIO: Rub him about the temples.

IAGO: No, forbear;
60   The lethargy must have his quiet course:
If not, he foams at mouth, and by and by
Breaks out to savage madness. Look, he stirs:
Do you withdraw yourself a little while,
He will recover straight. When he is gone,
65   I would on great occasion speak with you.   *[Exit Cassio.]*
How is it, general? Have you not hurt your head?

OTHELLO: Dost thou mock me?

IAGO: With her, on her, whatever you think.

OTHELLO: Lie with her! Lie on her! We say lie on her, when we mean lie with her. Lie with her! That's disgusting. Handkerchief—confessions—handkerchief! To confess, and be hanged for his pains. First to be hanged, and then to confess.—I tremble at the thought. My nature would not lead me to such anger for no reason. It is not words that upset me like this. Pish! Noses, ears, and lips. Is it possible?—Confess?—handkerchief!—Oh, devil!

[Falls into a trance]

IAGO: [Aside] Continue working; my plan to poison Othello's thoughts is working! This is how gullible fools are caught. And even many worthy and honest women, who are entirely guiltless, are punished. What, ho! My lord! My lord, I say! Othello!

[Enter Cassio]
Hello, Cassio!

CASSIO: What's the matter?

IAGO: My lord has fallen into an epileptic seizure. This is his second fit. He had one yesterday.

CASSIO: Rub his temples.

IAGO: No, leave him alone. The coma must run its course. If it doesn't, he will foam at the mouth and eventually break into a fit of wild madness. Look! He stirs. Go away for a little while; he will recover soon. When he has gone home, I will speak with you. [Exit Cassio] How are you, general? Have you hurt your head?

OTHELLO: Are you making fun of me?

IAGO: I mock you? No, by heaven.
    Would you would bear your fortune like a man!

70   OTHELLO: A horned man's a monster and a beast.

IAGO: There's many a beast then in a populous city,
    And many a civil monster.

OTHELLO: Did he confess it?

IAGO: Good sir, be a man;
75   Think every bearded fellow that's but yoked
    May draw with you. There's millions now alive
    That nightly lie in those unproper beds
    Which they dare swear peculiar. Your case is better.
    O, 'tis the spite of hell, the fiend's archmock,
80   To lip a wanton in a secure couch,
    And to suppose her chaste! No, let me know;
    And knowing what I am, I know what she shall be.

OTHELLO: O, thou art wise; 'tis certain.

IAGO: Stand you awhile apart;
85   Confine yourself but in a patient list.
    Whilst you were here o'erwhelmed with your grief—
    A passion most unsuiting such a man—
    Cassio came hither. I shifted him away,
    And laid good 'scuse upon your ecstasy;
90   Bade him anon return and here speak with me;
    The which he promised. Do but encave yourself,
    And mark the fleers, the gibes, and notable scorns,
    That dwell in every region of his face;
    For I will make him tell the tale anew,
95   Where, how, how oft, how long ago, and when
    He hath and is again to cope your wife:
    I say, but mark his gesture. Marry, patience,
    Or I shall say you are all in all in spleen,
    And nothing of a man.

IAGO: *Make fun of you? No, by heaven. I wish you would bear your fate like a man!*

OTHELLO: *An adulterer is a monster and a beast.*

IAGO: *Then there are many beasts in a populous city and many polite monsters.*

OTHELLO: *Has he confessed?*

IAGO: *Good sir, be a man. Remember that every cuckold in the same situation stands with you. Every night, there are millions of people who lie in an indecent bed claiming that it is their own. Your situation is better. Oh, it is the ill will of hell, the devil's main joke, to kiss a whore in a hidden place, and think that she is chaste! No, let me know; knowing what I am, I know what she will be.*

OTHELLO: *Oh, you are wise, it is certain.*

IAGO: *Keep your distance for a while; confine yourself and be patient. While you were here overwhelmed with grief—an outburst most unbecoming to a man like yourself—Cassio came here. I pushed him away and made up a good excuse for your trance. I told him to come back shortly to speak with me; he promised to do so. Hide in a spot where you can see him and watch his sneers, the jokes, and the obvious hatred that dwells in every part of his face. I will make him tell the story again. Where, how, how often, how long ago, when he has in the past, and when he is going to join with your wife again. I say, notice his gestures. Be patient, or I will say you are all emotions and not a man.*

100 OTHELLO: Dost thou hear, Iago?
　　　　I will be found most cunning in my patience;
　　　　But—dost thou hear?—most bloody.

　　IAGO: That's not amiss;
　　　　But yet keep time in all. Will you withdraw?
　　　　　　　　　　　　　　　　[Othello retires.]
105　　Now will I question Cassio of Bianca,
　　　　A housewife that by selling her desires
　　　　Buys herself bread and clothes. It is a creature
　　　　That dotes on Cassio, as 'tis the strumpet's plague
　　　　To beguile many and be beguiled by one.
110　　He, when he hears of her, cannot refrain
　　　　From the excess of laughter. Here he comes.
　　　　As he shall smile, Othello shall go mad;
　　　　And his unbookish jealousy must construe
　　　　Poor Cassio's smiles, gestures, and light behavior,
115　　Quite in the wrong. How do you now, lieutenant?

　　[Reenter Cassio]

　　CASSIO: The worser that you give me the addition
　　　　Whose want even kills me.

　　IAGO: Ply Desdemona well, and you are sure on't.
　　　　Now, if this suit lay in Bianca's power,
120　　How quickly should you speed!

　　CASSIO: Alas, poor caitiff!

　　OTHELLO: Look, how he laughs already!

　　IAGO: I never knew a woman love man so.

　　CASSIO: Alas, poor rogue! I think, i'faith, she loves me.

125　OTHELLO: Now he denies it faintly and laughs it out.

OTHELLO: *Listen, Iago! You will find I am very good at being patient; but—do you understand—also extremely bloody.*

IAGO: *That is not bad. But be patient. Will you hide?* [Othello retires] *Now I will ask Cassio questions about Bianca, a housewife who sells pleasures to buy bread and clothes. This woman loves Cassio, and she suffers from the prostitute's disease of charming many and being charmed by one. When Cassio hears about her, he cannot stop himself from laughing. Here he comes. While he smiles, Othello will go mad and his ignorant jealousy will seriously misinterpret poor Cassio's smiles, gestures, and light behavior. How goes it, lieutenant?*

[Reenter Cassio]

CASSIO: *It's worse because you call me by a title that I would die to have back.*

IAGO: *Convince Desdemona, and you are guaranteed to have it back.* [Speaking lower, so that Othello cannot hear] *Now, if this situation was in Bianca's power to fix, how quickly would you succeed!*

CASSIO: *Alas, the poor wretch!*

OTHELLO: *Look, at how he laughs already!*

IAGO: *I never knew a woman could love a man so much.*

CASSIO: *Alas, poor thing! Honestly, I think she loves me.*

OTHELLO: *Now he weakly denies it, and laughs it off.*

177

IAGO: Do you hear, Cassio?

OTHELLO: Now he importunes him
　　To tell it o'er. Go to; well said, well said.

IAGO: She gives it out that you shall marry her;
130　　Do you intend it?

CASSIO: Ha, ha, ha!

OTHELLO: Do you triumph, Roman? Do you triumph?

CASSIO: I marry her! What? A customer! I prithee, bear some charity
　　to my wit; do not think it so unwholesome. Ha, ha, ha!

135　OTHELLO: So, so, so, so. They laugh that win.

IAGO: Faith, the cry goes that you shall marry her.

CASSIO: Prithee, say true.

IAGO: I am a very villain else.

OTHELLO: Have you scored me? Well.

140　CASSIO: This is the monkey's own giving out. She is persuaded I will
　　marry her, out of her own love and flattery, not out of my promise.

OTHELLO: Iago beckons me; now he begins the story.

CASSIO: She was here even now; she haunts me in every place. I was
　　the other day talking on the sea bank with certain Venetians, and
145　　thither comes the bauble, and, by this hand, she falls me thus about
　　my neck—

OTHELLO: Crying, "O dear Cassio!" as it were; his gesture imports it.

IAGO: *Do you hear, Cassio?*

OTHELLO: *Now Iago urges Cassio to tell the whole story. Go on; well said, well said.*

IAGO: *Bianca says that you two are going to get married. Do you intend to marry her?*

CASSIO: *Ha, ha, ha!*

OTHELLO: *Do you win, Roman? Do you win?*

CASSIO: *I marry her! What? I am her customer! I beg you, give me some credit; do not think I am that stupid. Ha, ha, ha!*

OTHELLO: *So, so, so, so. They laugh at that win.*

IAGO: *It's true; the story is that you will marry her.*

CASSIO: *I beg you, be honest.*

IAGO: *If I'm not, I am an absolute villain.*

OTHELLO: *Have you wounded me? Well.*

CASSIO: *This is the monkey's version of the truth. She thinks I will marry her because of her own love and flattery, not because of my promise.*

OTHELLO: *Iago signaled me. Cassio is beginning the story now.*

CASSIO: *She was here just now; she follows me everywhere. The other day, I was talking with some Venetians on the sea bank; and there comes the plaything, and, I swear, she grabbed me around my neck, like this—*

OTHELLO: *Crying "Oh, dear Cassio!" You can tell from his gesture.*

CASSIO: So hangs and lolls and weeps upon me; so hales and pulls me. Ha, ha, ha!

150 OTHELLO: Now he tells how she plucked him to my chamber. O, I see that nose of yours, but not that dog I shall throw it to.

CASSIO: Well, I must leave her company.

IAGO: Before me! look where she comes.

CASSIO: 'Tis such another fitchew! marry, a perfumed one.

[Enter Bianca.]
155   What do you mean by this haunting of me?

BIANCA: Let the devil and his dam haunt you! What did you mean by that same handkerchief you gave me even now? I was a fine fool to take it. I must take out the work? A likely piece of work that you should find it in your chamber and not know who left it there! This
160   is some minx's token, and I must take out the work? There, give it your hobbyhorse. Wheresoever you had it, I'll take out no work on't.

CASSIO: How now, my sweet Bianca! how now! how now!

OTHELLO: By heaven, that should be my handkerchief!

165 BIANCA: An you'll come to supper tonight, you may; an you will not, come when you are next prepared for.   *[Exit.]*

IAGO: After her, after her.

CASSIO: Faith, I must; she'll rail i' the street else.

IAGO: Will you sup there?

CASSIO: *So she hangs and leans against me; then she cries and pulls on me. Ha, ha, ha!*

OTHELLO: *Now he is telling about how she dragged him to my bedroom. Oh, I see what you've done, and I am plotting my revenge; but the time is not quite right.*

CASSIO: *Well, I must stop spending time with her.*

IAGO: *Look, here she comes.*

CASSIO: *It is just another whore! Yes, one that smells perfumed.*

[Enter Bianca]
Why are you stalking me like this?

BIANCA: *Let the devil and his mother stalk you! What was the idea giving me that handkerchief? I was a perfect fool to take it. I must copy it? I'm sure you found it in your apartment and don't know who left it there! This is some girlfriend's gift, and I must copy it? Here give it to your whore; wherever you got it from, I will not copy it.*

CASSIO: *Now now, my sweet Bianca! Now now! Now now!*

OTHELLO: *Oh my heaven, that is my handkerchief!*

BIANCA: *If you would like to come to dinner tonight, you may; but, if not, you can come when you're ready.*   [Exit]

IAGO: *Go after her! After her.*

CASSIO: *Honestly, I must go after her, or else she'll holler in the street.*

IAGO: *Will you eat supper there?*

181

170   CASSIO: Faith, I intend so.

IAGO: Well, I may chance to see you, for I would very fain speak with you.

CASSIO: Prithee, come; will you?

IAGO: Go to; say no more.   *[Exit Cassio.]*

175   OTHELLO: *[Advancing.]* How shall I murder him, Iago?

IAGO: Did you perceive how he laughed at his vice?

OTHELLO: O Iago!

IAGO: And did you see the handkerchief?

OTHELLO: Was that mine?

180   IAGO: Yours, by this hand. And to see how he prizes the foolish woman your wife! She gave it him, and he hath given it his whore.

OTHELLO: I would have him nine years akilling. A fine woman! a fair woman! a sweet woman!

IAGO: Nay, you must forget that.

185   OTHELLO: Ay, let her rot, and perish, and be damned tonight, for she shall not live. No, my heart is turned to stone; I strike it, and it hurts my hand. O, the world hath not a sweeter creature. She might lie by an emperor's side, and command him tasks.

IAGO: Nay, that's not your way.

190   OTHELLO: Hang her! I do but say what she is. So delicate with her needle, an admirable musician. O, she will sing the savageness out of a bear. Of so high and plenteous wit and invention!

ACT IV SCENE 1

CASSIO: *Yes, I intend to.*

IAGO: *Well, I might see you later then because I would like to speak with you.*

CASSIO: *Please come for dinner, will you?*

IAGO: *Go on; and do not say anything more.*   [Exit Cassio]

OTHELLO: [Advancing] *How should I murder him, Iago?*

IAGO: *Did you see how he laughed at his wickedness?*

OTHELLO: *Oh, Iago!*

IAGO: *And did you see the handkerchief?*

OTHELLO: *Was that mine?*

IAGO: *Yours, I swear to it. And do you see how he values the foolish woman, your wife! She gave it to him, and he has given it to his whore.*

OTHELLO: *I wish I could spend nine years killing him. A fine woman! A fair woman! A sweet woman!*

IAGO: *No, you must forget that.*

OTHELLO: *Yes, let her rot and perish and be damned tonight, because she will die. No, my heart has turned to stone, and when I hit it, it hurts my hand. Oh, the world does not have a sweeter creature. She could lie by an emperor's side and order him about.*

IAGO: *No, don't think that way.*

OTHELLO: *Hang her! I am only saying what she really is. She is a skilled seamstress and an extraordinary musician. Her singing could tame a bear. She has so much refined intelligence and imagination—*

IAGO: She's the worse for all this.

OTHELLO: O, a thousand, a thousand times. And then, of so gentle a
195   condition!

IAGO: Ay, too gentle.

OTHELLO: Nay, that's certain. But yet the pity of it, Iago! O Iago, the
pity of it, Iago!

IAGO: If you are so fond over her iniquity, give her patent to offend, for,
200   if it touch not you, it comes near nobody.

OTHELLO: I will chop her into messes. Cuckold me!

IAGO: O, 'tis foul in her.

OTHELLO: With mine officer!

IAGO: That's fouler.

205   OTHELLO: Get me some poison, Iago, this night. I'll not expostulate
with her, lest her body and beauty unprovide my mind again. This
night, Iago:

IAGO: Do it not with poison, strangle her in her bed, even the bed she
hath contaminated.

210   OTHELLO: Good, good, the justice of it pleases, very good.

IAGO: And for Cassio, let me be his undertaker. You shall hear more by
midnight.

OTHELLO: Excellent good. *[A trumpet within.]* What trumpet is that
same?

215   IAGO: Something from Venice, sure. 'Tis Lodovico
Come from the Duke. And, see your wife is with him.

IAGO: She's worse for putting you through this.

OTHELLO: Oh, a thousand, a thousand times worse. And yet she has such a gentle disposition!

IAGO: Yes, too gentle.

OTHELLO: Now, that's certain. But the pity of it, Iago! Oh, Iago, the pity of it, Iago!

IAGO: If you love her crime so much, give her permission to sin against you. If it doesn't bother you, it is nobody else's business.

OTHELLO: I will chop her into pieces for making a cuckold out of me!

IAGO: Oh, It is disgusting of her.

OTHELLO: With my own officer!

IAGO: That's even worse.

OTHELLO: Get me some poison tonight, Iago. I will not argue at length with her, because I fear that her body and beauty will change my mind again. Tonight, Iago.

IAGO: Don't do it with poison; strangle her in her bed, the very bed she has contaminated.

OTHELLO: Good, good. I like the justice of it, very good.

IAGO: As for Cassio, let me deal with him. You will hear more by midnight.

OTHELLO: Very good. [A trumpet within] What trumpet is that?

IAGO: Something from Venice, I'm sure. It is Lodovico, who was sent by the Duke. And look, your wife is with him.

[Enter Lodovico, Desdemona, and Attendants.]

LODOVICO: God save the worthy general!

OTHELLO: With all my heart, sir.

LODOVICO: The Duke and Senators of Venice greet you.
[Gives him a letter.]

220   OTHELLO: I kiss the instrument of their pleasures.
[Opens the letter, and reads.]

DESD: And what's the news, good cousin Lodovico?

IAGO: I am very glad to see you, signior. Welcome to Cyprus.

LODOVICO: I thank you. How does Lieutenant Cassio?

IAGO: Lives, sir.

225   DESD: Cousin, there's fall'n between him and my lord
An unkind breech; but you shall make all well.

OTHELLO: Are you sure of that?

DESD: My lord?

OTHELLO: *[Reads.]* "This fail you not to do, as you will"

230   LODOVICO: He did not call; he's busy in the paper.
Is there division 'twixt my lord and Cassio?

DESD: A most unhappy one. I would do much
To atone them, for the love I bear to Cassio:

OTHELLO: Fire and brimstone!

[Enter Lodovico, Desdemona, and Attendants]

LODOVICO: *God save you, worthy general!*

OTHELLO: *I welcome you with all my heart, sir.*

LODOVICO: *The Duke and Senators of Venice say hello.*
[Gives Othello a letter]

OTHELLO: *I thank the messenger who brings their commands.*
[Opens the letter, and reads]

DESD: *What's is this news, good cousin Lodovico?*

IAGO: *I am very glad to see you, sir. Welcome to Cyprus.*

LODOVICO: *Thank you. How is Lieutenant Cassio?*

IAGO: *He is alive, sir.*

DESD: *Cousin, there has been a dispute between Cassio and my lord. An unpleasant breakup, but you will make it well again.*

OTHELLO: *Are you sure of that?*

DESD: *My lord?*

OTHELLO: [Continues reading letter] *"Do not fail to do this, as you will"*—

LODOVICO: [To Desdemona] *Othello did not say anything; he is busy reading the paper. Has there been a dispute between my lord and Cassio?*

DESD: *A very miserable one. I will do all I can to get them together because of the love I have for Cassio.*

OTHELLO: [Her last comment stirs him] *Fire and brimstone!*

235 DESD: My lord?

OTHELLO: Are you wise?

DESD: What, is he angry?

LODOVICO: May be the letter moved him;
For, as I think, they do command him home,
240   Deputing Cassio in his government.

DESD: By my troth, I am glad on't.

OTHELLO: Indeed!

DESD: My lord?

OTHELLO: I am glad to see you mad.

245 DESD: Why, sweet Othello?

OTHELLO: Devil! *[Strikes her.]*

DESD: I have not deserved this.

LODOVICO: My lord, this would not be believed in Venice,
Though I should swear I saw't. 'Tis very much:
250   Make her amends; she weeps.

OTHELLO: O devil, devil!
If that the earth could teem with woman's tears,
Each drop she falls would prove a crocodile.
Out of my sight!

255 DESD: *[Going.]* I will not stay to offend you.

LODOVICO: Truly, an obedient lady:
I do beseech your lordship, call her back.

DESD: *My lord?*

OTHELLO: [Angrily] *Are you being disrespectful?*

DESD: *What, is he angry?*

LODOVICO: *Maybe something in the letter upset him. I think they are ordering him to come home, authorizing Cassio to replace him as governor.*

DESD: *Trust me, I am pleased about that.*

OTHELLO: *Indeed!*

DESD: *My lord?*

OTHELLO: *I am glad to see you are wanton.*

DESD: *Why, sweet Othello?*

OTHELLO: [Striking her] *Devil!*

DESD: *I do not deserve this.*

LODOVICO: *My lord, the people of Venice will not believe this, even though I can swear I saw it. This is terrible. Apologize to her; she is crying.*

OTHELLO: *Oh, devil, devil! If the earth was flooded with woman's tears, each drop she cries would prove to be false. Get out of my sight!*

DESD: [Going] *I will not stay here and continue to offend you.*

LODOVICO: *She is truly an obedient lady. I will ask you, my lord, call her back.*

OTHELLO: Mistress!

DESD: My lord?

260 OTHELLO: What would you with her, sir?

LODOVICO: Who, I, my lord?

OTHELLO: Ay, you did wish that I would make her turn:
Sir, she can turn and turn, and yet go on,
And turn again; and she can weep, sir, weep;
265 And she's obedient, as you say, obedient,
Very obedient. Proceed you in your tears.
Concerning this, sir—O well-painted passion!—
I am commanded home. Get you away;
I'll send for you anon. Sir, I obey the mandate,
270 And will return to Venice. Hence, avaunt!
[Exit Desdemona.]
Cassio shall have my place. And, sir, tonight,
I do entreat that we may sup together.
You are welcome, sir, to Cyprus. Goats and monkeys!
[Exit.]

LODOVICO: Is this the noble Moor whom our full Senate
275 Call all in all sufficient? This the nature
Whom passion could not shake? whose solid virtue
The shot of accident nor dart of chance
Could neither graze nor pierce?

IAGO: He is much changed.

280 LODOVICO: Are his wits safe? Is he not light of brain?

IAGO: He's that he is. I may not breathe my censure
What he might be: if what he might he is not,
I would to heaven he were!

OTHELLO: *Mistress!*

DESD: *My lord?*

OTHELLO: *What do you want her for, sir?*

LODOVICO: *Who, me, my lord?*

OTHELLO: *Yes. You wanted me to make her turn around. Sir, she can turn and turn, leave again, and turn again, and she can cry, sir, cry. She's obedient, like you said, very obedient. Keep crying. In regards to this, sir,—Oh, well-disguised sorrow!—I am ordered home. Get away from me, I'll send for you shortly. Sir, I will obey the order, and will return to Venice. Go—Get out of here!*

[Exit Desdemona]

Cassio will take my place. And, sir, tonight, I invite you to eat with me. You are welcome, sir, to Cyprus. Goats and monkeys!

[Exit]

LODOVICO: *Is this the same noble Moor whom our whole Senate says is unmatched? Is this the same character that passion cannot overpower, the same man whose solid, strong integrity cannot be damaged by anything?*

IAGO: *He has changed a great deal.*

LODOVICO: *Is he sane? Is he going slightly insane?*

IAGO: *He is what he is. I will not say anything bad about how he might be. However, what he might be–if what he might be, he is not– I wish to heaven he were.*

LODOVICO: What, strike his wife!

285 IAGO: Faith, that was not so well; yet would I knew
    That stroke would prove the worst!

LODOVICO: Is it his use?
    Or did the letters work upon his blood,
    And new create this fault?

290 IAGO: Alas, alas!
    It is not honesty in me to speak
    What I have seen and known. You shall observe him,
    And his own courses will denote him so
    That I may save my speech: do but go after,
295   And mark how he continues.

LODOVICO: I am sorry that I am deceived in him.

[Exeunt.]

SCENE 2
A room in the castle.

[Enter Othello and Emilia.]

OTHELLO: You have seen nothing, then?

EMILIA: Nor ever heard, nor ever did suspect.

OTHELLO: Yes, you have seen Cassio and she together.

EMILIA: But then I saw no harm, and then I heard
5   Each syllable that breath made up between them.

OTHELLO: What, did they never whisper?

192

LODOVICO: He struck his wife!

IAGO: In truth, that was not so good; I wish I knew if hitting her will be the worst of it!

LODOVICO: Is he usually like this, or did the letters get him worked up and create this problem?

IAGO: Alas, alas! I do not think it is right for me to say what I have seen and known. Watch him, and his actions will reveal who he is so that I do not need to talk about it. But, go after him, and notice how he acts.

LODOVICO: I am sorry that I was wrong about him.

[Exeunt]

SCENE 2
A room in the castle.

[Enter Othello and Emilia]

OTHELLO: You have not seen anything then?

EMILIA: Nor heard anything or had any suspicions.

OTHELLO: Yes, but you have seen Cassio and her together.

EMILIA: But I saw no harm, and I heard each syllable that was spoken between them.

OTHELLO: They never whispered?

EMILIA: Never, my lord.

OTHELLO: Nor send you out o' the way?

EMILIA: Never.

10 OTHELLO: To fetch her fan, her gloves, her mask, nor nothing?

EMILIA: Never, my lord.

OTHELLO: That's strange.

EMILIA: I durst, my lord, to wager she is honest,
      Lay down my soul at stake. If you think other,
15   Remove your thought; it doth abuse your bosom.
      If any wretch have put this in your head,
      Let heaven requite it with the serpent's curse!
      For if she be not honest, chaste, and true,
      There's no man happy; the purest of their wives
20   Is foul as slander.

OTHELLO: Bid her come hither; go.   *[Exit Emilia.]*
      She says enough; yet she's a simple bawd
      That cannot say as much. This is a subtle whore,
      A closet lock and key of villainous secrets:
25   And yet she'll kneel and pray; I have seen her do't.

[Enter Desdemona with Emilia.]

DESD: My lord, what is your will?

OTHELLO: Pray, chuck, come hither.

DESD: What is your pleasure?

OTHELLO: Let me see your eyes; Look in my face.

EMILIA: *Never, my lord.*

OTHELLO: *They never sent you out of the room?*

EMILIA: *Never.*

OTHELLO: *To fetch her fan, her gloves, her mask, or anything?*

EMILIA: *Never, my lord.*

OTHELLO: *That is strange.*

EMILIA: *I would bet anything, my lord, that she is faithful. I'll bet my soul. If you think otherwise, you should throw away that thought. It is hurting your heart. If any wretch has put these thoughts into your head, let heaven punish him with the serpent's curse! If she is not faithful, honest, and true, then no one's wife is. Then, the purest wife is as evil as a dishonorable deed.*

OTHELLO: *Ask her to come here. Go.*   [Exit Emilia]
   She says enough; yet she's a simple girl that cannot say much. Desdemona is a sneaky whore; she has a locked closet full of villainous secrets, but she still kneels and prays. I have seen her do it.

[Enter Desdemona with Emilia]

DESD: *My lord, what do you need?*

OTHELLO: *Please, dear, come here.*

DESD: *What would you like?*

OTHELLO: *Let me see your eyes. Look in my face.*

30   DESD: What horrible fancy's this?

      OTHELLO: *[To Emilia.]* Some of your function, mistress,
            Leave procreants alone and shut the door;
            Cough, or cry "hem," if anybody come:
            Your mystery, your mystery; nay, dispatch.

                                              [Exit Emilia.]

35   DESD: Upon my knees, what doth your speech import?
            I understand a fury in your words,
            But not the words.

      OTHELLO: Why, what art thou?

      DESD: Your wife, my lord, your true and loyal wife.

40   OTHELLO: Come, swear it, damn thyself;
            Lest, being like one of heaven, the devils themselves
            Should fear to seize thee. Therefore be doubledamn'd;
            Swear thou art honest.

      DESD: Heaven doth truly know it.

45   OTHELLO: Heaven truly knows that thou art false as hell.

      DESD: To whom, my lord? with whom? how am I false?

      OTHELLO: O Desdemona! Away! away! away!

      DESD: Alas the heavy day! Why do you weep?
            Am I the motive of these tears, my lord?
50   If haply you my father do suspect
            An instrument of this your calling back,
            Lay not your blame on me. If you have lost him:
            Why, I have lost him too.

      OTHELLO: Had it pleased heaven

DESD: *What kind of horrible desire do you have?*

OTHELLO: *To see what you do.* [To Emilia] *Your job is to watch the door, mistress, and leave us lovers alone and shut the door. Cough, or cry, "hem," if anybody comes around. Your trade. Your profession. Now, go.*

[Exit Emilia]

DESD: *I am down on my knees. What are you trying to say? I sense anger behind your words, but not the words themselves.*

OTHELLO: *Why, what are you?*

DESD: *Your wife, my lord, your faithful and loyal wife.*

OTHELLO: *Come, swear it; damn yourself. Otherwise, because you are an angel, the devils themselves will be afraid to seize you. Therefore, double damn yourself. Swear that you are faithful.*

DESD: *Heaven truly knows it.*

OTHELLO: *Heaven truly knows that you are as unfaithful as hell.*

DESD: *To whom, my lord? With whom? How am I unfaithful?*

OTHELLO: *Oh, Desdemona! Away! Away! Away!*

DESD: *Alas this terrible day! Why do you cry? Have I caused these tears, my lord? Perhaps you suspect my father has played some part in calling you back to Venice; do not blame me. If you have given up on him, well then, I have given up on him too.*

OTHELLO: *If heaven wanted to test me with hardships by showering me with all*

55   To try me with affliction; had they rain'd
    All kinds of sores and shames on my bare head,
    Steep'd me in poverty to the very lips,
    Given to captivity me and my utmost hopes,
    I should have found in some place of my soul
60   A drop of patience; but, alas, to make me
    A fixed figure for the time of scorn
    To point his slow unmoving finger at!
    Yet could I bear that too, well, very well;
    But there, where I have garner'd up my heart,
65   Where either I must live or bear no life;
    The fountain from the which my current runs,
    Or else dries up; to be discarded thence!
    Or keep it as a cistern for foul toads
    To knot and gender in! Turn thy complexion there,
70   Patience, thou young and roselipp'd cherubin,
    Ay, there, look grim as hell!

DESD: I hope my noble lord esteems me honest.

OTHELLO: O, ay, as summer flies are in the shambles,
    That quicken even with blowing. O thou weed,
75   Who art so lovely fair and smell'st so sweet
    That the sense aches at thee, would thou hadst ne'er been born!

DESD: Alas, what ignorant sin have I committed?

OTHELLO: Was this fair paper, this most goodly book,
    Made to write "whore" upon? What committed?
80   Committed! O thou public commoner!
    I should make very forges of my cheeks,
    That would to cinders burn up modesty,
    Did I but speak thy deeds. What committed!
    Heaven stops the nose at it, and the moon winks;
85   The bawdy wind, that kisses all it meets,
    Is hush'd within the hollow mine of earth,
    And will not hear it. What committed.
    Impudent strumpet!

kinds of sorrows and scandals on my head, flooded me with poverty up to my lips, and locked me and my hopes up in prison, then I would have found within myself a drop of patience. But, alas, to make me a laughing stock, a man whom scorn points at with a slow unmoving finger– I could stand even that well, very well. But in you, I have stored my heart. I will live or die by you; you are the fountain from which my life flows, or dries up to be thrown away by you! Or should I keep it as a tub for foul toads to have sex in! Turn your face this way. Patience, you young and rose-lipped angel,—Yes, there, look as grim as hell!

DESD: I hope my noble lord knows that I am faithful.

OTHELLO: Oh, yes; as faithful as summer flies that are in a slaughterhouse and become pregnant easily. Oh, you weed, who are so lovely, fair, and smells so sweet that you make my senses ache, I wish you had never been born!

DESD: What sin have I unknowingly committed?

OTHELLO: Why was "whore" written on this fair face, this good book? What sin have you committed? Committed! Oh, you public whore! If I say what you did, it will make fires come out of my cheeks and burn your fake modesty into cinders. What sin have you committed! Heaven holds its nose against it, and the moon closes its eyes. The lustful wind that kisses everything it meets, is quiet underground and will not listen to what you did. What sin have you committed! Shameless prostitute!

DESD: By heaven, you do me wrong.

90 OTHELLO: Are not you a strumpet?

DESD: No, as I am a Christian.
        If to preserve this vessel for my lord
        From any other foul unlawful touch
        Be not to be a strumpet, I am none.

95 OTHELLO: What, not a whore?

DESD: No, as I shall be saved.

OTHELLO: Is't possible?

DESD: O, heaven forgive us!

OTHELLO: I cry you mercy then;
100   I took you for that cunning whore of Venice
        That married with Othello. You, mistress,   *[Raises his voice.]*
        That have the office opposite to Saint Peter,
        And keep the gate of hell!

        [Reenter Emilia.]
        You, you, ay, you!
105   We have done our course; there's money for your pains. I pray you,
        turn the key, and keep our counsel.   *[Exit.]*

EMILIA: Alas, what does this gentleman conceive?
        How do you, madam? How do you, my good lady?

DESD: Faith, half asleep.

110 EMILIA: Good madam, what's the matter with my lord?

DESD: With who?

200

DESD: I swear by heaven, you are wrong about me.

OTHELLO: You are not a whore?

DESD: No, as a Christian, I swear. If protecting my body from any other foul, unlawful touching for you means that I am not a whore, then I am not one.

OTHELLO: What, not a whore?

DESD: No, I will be saved.

OTHELLO: Is it possible?

DESD: Oh, heaven forgive us!

OTHELLO: I apologize then. I thought you were that cunning whore of Venice who married Othello. You, mistress, who has the job opposite Saint Peter's—you are keeping the gate of hell!

[Reenter Emilia]
    You, you, yes, you! We are finished with our business. There's some money for your trouble. Please, turn the key and keep her company.
[Exit Othello]

EMILIA: Alas, what does this gentleman think? How are you, madam? How are you, my good lady?

DESD: Honestly, I'm half asleep.

EMILIA: Good madam, what is wrong with my lord?

DESD: With who?

EMILIA: Why, with my lord, madam.

DESD: Who is thy lord?

EMILIA: He that is yours, sweet lady.

115   DESD: I have none. Do not talk to me, Emilia;
         I cannot weep, nor answer have I none
         But what should go by water. Prithee, tonight
         Lay on my bed my wedding sheets. Remember;
         And call thy husband hither.

120   EMILIA: Here's a change indeed!   [Exit.]

      DESD: 'Tis meet I should be used so, very meet.
         How have I been behaved, that he might stick
         The small'st opinion on my least misuse?

[Reenter Emilia with Iago.]

IAGO: What is your pleasure, madam? How is't with you?

125   DESD: I cannot tell. Those that do teach young babes
         Do it with gentle means and easy tasks:
         He might have chid me so, for in good faith,
         I am a child to chiding.

IAGO: What's the matter, lady?

130   EMILIA: Alas, Iago, my lord hath so bewhored her,
         Thrown such despite and heavy terms upon her,
         As true hearts cannot bear.

      DESD: Am I that name, Iago?

IAGO: What name, fair lady?

EMILIA: *Why, with my lord, madam.*

DESD: *Who is your lord?*

EMILIA: *The man who is yours, sweet lady.*

DESD: *I have no lord. Do not talk to me, Emilia, I do not want to cry, and the only answers I can give are with tears. I beg you, tonight put my wedding sheets on my bed; remember, and tell your husband to come here.*

EMILIA: *Here's a change indeed!*   [Exit]

DESD: *It is fitting that I should be used like this, very fitting. How have I behaved that he will attach the worst suspicion to a minor mistake?*

[Reenter Emilia with Iago]

IAGO: *What can I do for you, madam? How are you?*

DESD: *I cannot say. People who teach babies to behave do it with gentle methods and easy tasks. He might have just scolded me in that way, for I am not used to being scolded.*

IAGO: *What's the matter, lady?*

EMILIA: *Alas, Iago, my lord has called her a whore. He has thrown such anger and serious names her that true friends cannot stand it.*

DESD: *Am I that name, Iago?*

IAGO: *What name, fair lady?*

135 DESD: Such as she says my lord did say I was.

EMILIA: He call'd her whore; a beggar in his drink
Could not have laid such terms upon his callet.

IAGO: Why did he so?

DESD: I do not know; I am sure I am none such.

140 IAGO: Do not weep, do not weep. Alas the day!

EMILIA: Hath she forsook so many noble matches,
Her father and her country and her friends,
To be call'd whore? Would it not make one weep?

DESD: It is my wretched fortune.

145 IAGO: How comes this trick upon him?

DESD: Nay, heaven doth know.

EMILIA: I will be hang'd, if some eternal villain,
Some busy and insinuating rogue,
Some cogging cozening slave, to get some office,
150   Have not devised this slander; I'll be hang'd else.

IAGO: Fie, there is no such man; it is impossible.

DESD: If any such there be, heaven pardon him!

EMILIA: A halter pardon him! And hell gnaw his bones!
Why should he call her whore? Who keeps her company?
155   What place? What time? What form? What likelihood?
The Moor's abused by some most villainous knave,
Some base notorious knave, some scurvy fellow.
O heaven, that such companions thou'ldst unfold,
And put in every honest hand a whip

DESD: *The name Emilia told you that my lord said I was.*

EMILIA: *He called her whore. A drunken beggar could not have called his wench such names.*

IAGO: *Why did he do that?*

DESD: *I do not know. I am sure that I am not one.*

IAGO: *Do not cry, do not cry. Alas the day!*

EMILIA: *Has she turned down so many noble suitors, and given up her father, her country, and her friends, only to be called whore? Isn't it enough to make anyone cry?*

DESD: *It is my terrible fate.*

IAGO: *Where did he get this idea?*

DESD: *Only heaven knows.*

EMILIA: *I would die if some evil villain, some meddlesome and insinuating rogue, some deceptive, cheating slave, did not make up this lie to get some job. I would die.*

IAGO: *Never. There is no such man. It is impossible.*

DESD: *If there is, heaven forgive him!*

EMILIA: *A noose should forgive him, and hell should gnaw his bones! Why would he call her whore? Who spends time with her? Where? When? How? What is the likelihood? The Moor has been deceived by some very villainous knave, some disgraceful, notorious knave, some despicable fellow. Oh, I wish heaven would reveal the liars, and put a whip in every honest hand to lash the rascals naked through the world, from the east to the west!*

160   To lash the rascals naked through the world
       Even from the east to the west!

IAGO: Speak within door.

EMILIA: O, fie upon them! Some such squire he was
       That turn'd your wit the seamy side without,
165   And made you to suspect me with the Moor.

IAGO: You are a fool; go to.

DESD: O good Iago,
       What shall I do to win my lord again?
       Good friend, go to him, for by this light of heaven,
170   I know not how I lost him. Here I kneel:
       If e'er my will did trespass 'gainst his love
       Either in discourse of thought or actual deed,
       Or that mine eyes, mine ears, or any sense,
       Delighted them in any other form,
175   Or that I do not yet, and ever did,
       And ever will, though he do shake me off
       To beggarly divorcement, love him dearly,
       Comfort forswear me! Unkindness may do much,
       And his unkindness may defeat my life,
180   But never taint my love. I cannot say "whore."
       It doth abhor me now I speak the word;
       To do the act that might the addition earn
       Not the world's mass of vanity could make me.

IAGO: I pray you, be content; 'tis but his humor:
185   The business of the state does him offense,
       And he does chide with you.

DESD: If 'twere no other—

IAGO: 'Tis but so, I warrant.   [Trumpets within.]
       Hark, how these instruments summon to supper!

IAGO: *Keep your voice down.*

EMILIA: *Oh, to hell with them! It was the same kind of person that turned your reason inside out and made you suspect that I was with the Moor.*

IAGO: *You are a fool. Get out of here.*

DESD: *Oh, Iago, what can I do to win my lord back again? Good friend, go to him; by the light of heaven, I do not know how I lost him. I kneel here. May I never have peace of mind again if I ever committed a crime against his love. If it was in speech, thought, or deed, if I ever admired another man with my eyes, ears, or other senses, if I ever took pleasure in anyone but him–but perhaps I do not yet, ever did, nor will ever, love him dearly (although now, he wants to get rid of me with a wretched divorce). Deny me divine comfort! Unkindness can do a lot; and his unkindness may ruin my life, but it will never affect my love. I cannot even say "whore." I hate to speak the word. Nothing in the world could make me do the act that might earn me that label. No amount of vanity could!*

IAGO: *I beg you, be content. It is only his bad mood. The business of the state is upsetting him, and he is taking it out on you.*

DESD: *If it were nothing else—*

IAGO: *It is only that, I promise.*   [Trumpets within]
       Listen, these instruments call us to supper! The messengers of Venice are

190 The messengers of Venice stay the meat:
  Go in, and weep not; all things shall be well.

        [Exeunt Desdemona and Emilia.]

 [Enter Roderigo]
 How now, Roderigo!

ROD: I do not find that thou dealest justly with me.

IAGO: What in the contrary?

195 ROD: Every day thou daffest me with some device, Iago; and rather, as
  it seems to me now, keepest from me all conveniency than suppli-
  est me with the least advantage of hope. I will indeed no longer
  endure it; nor am I yet persuaded to put up in peace what already
  I have foolishly suffered.

200 IAGO: Will you hear me, Roderigo?

 ROD: Faith, I have heard too much, for your words and performances
  are no kin together.

IAGO: You charge me most unjustly.

 ROD: With nought but truth. I have wasted myself out of my means.
205 The jewels you have had from me to deliver to Desdemona would
  half have corrupted a votarist. You have told me she hath received
  them and returned me expectations and comforts of sudden respect
  and acquaintance; but I find none.

IAGO: Well, go to, very well.

210 ROD: Very well! go to! I cannot go to, man; nor 'tis not very well. By
  this hand, I say 'tis very scurvy, and begin to find myself fopped in
  it.

IAGO: Very well.

waiting to eat. Go in, and don't cry. Everything will be well.

[Exit Desdemona and Emilia]

[Enter Roderigo]
How are you, Roderigo!

ROD: *I don't think that you are dealing with me fairly.*

IAGO: *What, makes you think so?*

ROD: *Every day you put me off with some excuse, Iago. And now it seems to me that you are keeping away from me at every opportunity and not giving me any hope. I will not take it any longer, and I am not going to just quietly put up with what I have already foolishly suffered.*

IAGO: *Will you listen to me, Roderigo?*

ROD: *To tell you the truth, I have listened to you too much. What you say and what you do are not related.*

IAGO: *You accuse me most unfairly.*

ROD: *I accuse you of nothing but the truth. I spent all of my money. The jewels you have taken from me to give to Desdemona would have corrupted a nun. You told me she has received them and said that I should expect her company, respect, and an introduction, but nothing has happened.*

IAGO: *Well, be patient. All is well.*

ROD: *All is well! Be patient! I cannot be patient, man. Everything is not very well. I swear this whole business is despicable, and I am beginning to believe you tricked me.*

IAGO: *Very well.*

Rod: I tell you 'tis not very well. I will make myself known to
215   Desdemona: If she will return me my jewels, I will give over my
suit and repent my unlawful solicitation; if not, assure yourself I
will seek satisfaction of you.

Iago: You have said now.

Rod: Ay, and said nothing but what I protest intendment of doing.

220   Iago: Why, now I see there's mettle in thee; and even from this instant
do build on thee a better opinion than ever before. Give me thy
hand, Roderigo Thou hast taken against me a most just exception;
but yet, I protest, have dealt most directly in thy affair.

Rod: It hath not appeared.

225   Iago: I grant indeed it hath not appeared, and your suspicion is not
without wit and judgement. But, Roderigo, if thou hast that in thee
indeed, which I have greater reason to believe now than ever, I
mean purpose, courage, and valor, this night show it; if thou the
next night following enjoy not Desdemona, take me from this
230   world with treachery and devise engines for my life.

Rod: Well, what is it? Is it within reason and compass?

Iago: Sir, there is especial commission come from Venice to depute
Cassio in Othello's place.

Rod: Is that true? Why then Othello and Desdemona return again to
235   Venice.

Iago: O, no; he goes into Mauritania, and takes away with him the fair
Desdemona, unless his abode be lingered here by some accident;
wherein none can be so determinate as the removing of Cassio.

Rod: How do you mean, removing of him?

ROD: *I tell you it is not very well. I will introduce myself to Desdemona. If she will return my jewels, I will give up pursuing her and apologize for my unlawful wooing. If she does not give me the jewels, you can be sure that I will seek compensation from you.*

IAGO: *You have finished now.*

ROD: *Yes, and I didn't say anything except what I intend to do.*

IAGO: *Why, now I see you have courage, and from now on I will think better of you. Give me your hand, Roderigo. You have made a good point against me. However, I insist that I have acted directly in your interest.*

ROD: *It does not appear that way.*

IAGO: *I admit that it does not appear that way, and you are right to have suspicions. But, Roderigo, if you have purpose, courage, and valor, and indeed I have reason to believe you do, tonight you need to show it more than ever. If you are not enjoying Desdemona's company by tomorrow night, snatch me from this world by torture and make plans to take my life.*

ROD: *Well, what do you want me to do? Is it within reason and possibility?*

IAGO: *Sir, there is a special command from Venice to promote Cassio to Othello's position.*

ROD: *Is that true? Oh, so Othello and Desdemona will return to Venice.*

IAGO: *Oh, no; he is going to Mauritania, and he will take the beautiful Desdemona with him, unless his stay here is extended by some accident, like the removal of Cassio.*

ROD: *What do you mean, the removal of him?*

240 IAGO: Why, by making him uncapable of Othello's place; knocking out his brains.

ROD: And that you would have me to do?

IAGO: Ay, if you dare do yourself a profit and a right. He sups tonight with a harlotry, and thither will I go to him. He knows not yet of
245 his honorable fortune. If you will watch his going thence, which his will fashion to fall out between twelve and one, you may take him at your pleasure; I will be near to second your attempt, and he shall fall between us. Come, stand not amazed at it, but go along with me; I will show you such a necessity in his death that you
250 shall think yourself bound to put it on him. It is now high supper-time, and the night grows to waste. About it.

ROD: I will hear further reason for this.

IAGO: And you shall be satisfied.

[Exeunt.]

SCENE 3
Another room in the castle.

[Enter Othello, Lodovico, Desdemona, Emilia, and Attendants.]

LODOVICO: I do beseech you, sir, trouble yourself no further.

OTHELLO: O, pardon me; 'twill do me good to walk.

LODOVICO: Madam, good night; I humbly thank your ladyship.

DESD: Your honor is most welcome.

5 OTHELLO: Will you walk, sir? O—Desdemona—

IAGO: Well, by making him unable to take Othello's place, by knocking his brains out.

ROD: And that is what you want me to do?

IAGO: Yes, if you dare do this justice for your own advantage. He eats tonight with a prostitute, and I am meeting him there. He doesn't know of his good fortune. If you will watch him go there, which will be between twelve and one, you can take him when you are ready. I will be near to help your attempt, and he will fall between us. Come, don't stand here stunned by the plan; go along with me. I will explain to you why it is important to kill him, and you will feel an obligation to do it. It is now suppertime, and we are wasting time. Let's go.

ROD: I must hear more of the reason for this.

IAGO: You will be satisfied on that point.

[Exeunt]

SCENE 3
Another room in the castle.

[Enter Othello, Lodovico, Desdemona, Emilia, and Attendants]

LODOVICO: I beg you, sir, do not go to any more trouble.

OTHELLO: Oh, excuse me; it will do me good to walk.

LODOVICO: Madam, good night. I humbly thank you.

DESD: Your are most welcome.

OTHELLO: Will you walk, sir? Oh—Desdemona,—

DESD: My lord?

OTHELLO: Get you to bed on the instant; I will be returned forthwith:
Dismiss your attendant there; look it be done.

DESD: I will, my lord.
                    [Exeunt Othello, Lodovico, and Attendants.]

10   EMILIA: How goes it now? He looks gentler than he did.

DESD: He says he will return incontinent:
He hath commanded me to go to bed,
And bade me to dismiss you.

EMILIA: Dismiss me?

15   DESD: It was his bidding; therefore, good Emilia,
Give me my nightly wearing, and adieu.
We must not now displease him.

EMILIA: I would you had never seen him!

DESD: So would not I. My love doth so approve him,
20   That even his stubbornness, his checks, his frowns—
Prithee, unpin me—have grace and favor in them.

EMILIA: I have laid those sheets you bade me on the bed.

DESD: All's one. Good faith, how foolish are our minds!
If I do die before thee, prithee shroud me
25   In one of those same sheets.

EMILIA: Come, come, you talk.

DESD: My mother had a maid call'd Barbar;
She was in love, and he she loved proved mad
And did forsake her. She had a song of "willow";

DESD: *My lord?*

OTHELLO: *Get to bed right away. I will be right back. Dismiss your attendant; make sure this is done.*

DESD: *I will, my lord.*

[Exit Othello, Lodovico, and Attendants]

EMILIA: *How is it going? He looks calmer than he did earlier.*

DESD: *He says he will return immediately. He has ordered me to go to bed and has told me to dismiss you.*

EMILIA: *Dismiss me?*

DESD: *It was his request. Therefore, good Emilia, give me my nightclothes, and good-bye. We must not anger him now.*

EMILIA: *I wish you had never seen him!*

DESD: *I do not wish the same thing. I love him so much that even his stubbornness, his punishments, his frowns—Please, Emilia, unpin me—are attractive to me.*

EMILIA: *I have laid those sheets on the bed as you asked me to.*

DESD: *It doesn't matter. Honestly, how foolish are our minds! If I die before you, please, cover me in one of those same sheets.*

EMILIA: *Come, come, don't talk like that.*

DESD: *My mother had a maid named Barbary. She was in love, and the man she loved turned out to be crazy and deserted her. She sang a song about unhappy love. It was an old song, but it expressed her fate, and she died*

30 An old thing 'twas, but it express'd her fortune,
 And she died singing it. That song tonight
 Will not go from my mind; I have much to do
 But to go hang my head all at one side
 And sing it like poor Barbary. Prithee, dispatch.

35 EMILIA: Shall I go fetch your nightgown?

DESD: No, unpin me here.
 This Lodovico is a proper man.

EMILIA: A very handsome man.

DESD: He speaks well.

40 EMILIA: I know a lady in Venice would have walked barefoot to Palestine for a touch of his nether lip.

DESD: *[Sings.]* "The poor soul sat sighing by a sycamore tree,
  Sing all a green willow;
 Her hand on her bosom, her head on her knee,
45 Sing willow, willow, willow.
 The fresh streams ran by her, and murmur'd her moans;
  Sing willow, willow, willow;
 Her salt tears fell from her, and soften'd the stones"—
 Lay by these:—
50 Sing willow, willow, willow"
 Prithee, hie thee; he'll come anon:—
  "Sing all a green willow must be my garland.
  Let nobody blame him; his scorn I approve"
 Nay, that's not next. Hark, who is't that knocks?

55 EMILIA: It's the wind.

DESD: *[Sings.]* "I call'd my love false love; but what said he then?
  Sing willow, willow, willow:
 If I court moe women, you'll couch with moe men"

216

singing it. I can't get that song out of my mind tonight. I have a lot to do, but all I can do is hang my head to one side, and sing it like poor Barbary. Please be quick.

EMILIA: Should I go get your nightgown?

DESD: No, unpin me here. That Lodovico is a gentleman.

EMILIA: A very handsome man.

DESD: He's very articulate.

EMILIA: I know a lady in Venice who would have walked barefoot to Palestine to kiss his lips.

DESD: [Singing] "The poor soul sat sighing by a sycamore tree,
        Sing all a green willow.
    Her hand on her bosom, her head on her knee,
        Sing willow, willow, willow.
    The fresh streams ran by her, and murmured her moans;
        Sing willow, willow, willow;
    Her salt tears fell from her, and softened the stones"—
Lay by these:
    "Sing willow, willow, willow"
I beg you, please hurry; he'll be here soon.
    "Sing all a green willow must be my garland.
    Let nobody blame him; his scorn I approve"
No, that's not next. Listen! Who is knocking?

EMILIA: It's the wind.

DESD: [Continues singing] "I called my love false love; but what said he then?
        Sing willow, willow, willow:
    If I court more women, you'll couch with more men"

217

So get thee gone; good night. Mine eyes do itch;
60   Doth that bode weeping?

EMILIA: 'Tis neither here nor there.

DESD: I have heard it said so. O, these men, these men!
     Dost thou in conscience think—tell me, Emilia—
     That there be women do abuse their husbands
65   In such gross kind?

EMILIA: There be some such, no question.

DESD: Wouldst thou do such a deed for all the world?

EMILIA: Why, would not you?

DESD: No, by this heavenly light!

70   EMILIA: Nor I neither by this heavenly light; I might do't as well i' the
     dark.

DESD: Wouldst thou do such a deed for all the world?

EMILIA: The world's a huge thing; it is a great price
     For a small vice.

75   DESD: In troth, I think thou wouldst not.

EMILIA: In troth, I think I should, and undo't when I had done. Marry,
     I would not do such a thing for a jointring, nor for measures of
     lawn, nor for gowns, petticoats, nor caps, nor any petty exhibition;
     but, for the whole world why, who would not make her husband a
80   cuckold to make him a monarch? I should venture purgatory for't.

DESD: Beshrew me, if I would do such a wrong
     For the whole world.

Leave now, good night. My eyes itch; does that mean I am going to start crying?

EMILIA: *It doesn't mean anything.*

DESD: *I've heard that it does. Oh, these men, these men! Do you honestly think—tell me, Emilia,—that there are women who deceive their husbands in such a shameful way?*

EMILIA: *There are some such women, undoubtedly.*

DESD: *Would you do such a deed for the entire world?*

EMILIA: *Why, wouldn't you?*

DESD: *No, I swear!*

EMILIA: *Neither would I in this heavenly light; however, I might do it in the dark.*

DESD: *You would do such a deed for all of the world?*

EMILIA: *The world's a huge thing. It is a great prize, for a small evil.*

DESD: *In truth, I don't think you would.*

EMILIA: *In truth, I think I would; and then I'd undo it when I was done. I would not do it for a small token, nor for fine linen, or gowns, petticoats, caps, or any petty display of wealth. But for the whole world, why, who would not make her husband a cuckold to make him a king? I would risk purgatory for it.*

DESD: *Curse me, if I would do such a wrong for the whole world.*

219

EMILIA: Why, the wrong is but a wrong i' the world; and having the world for your labor, 'tis a wrong in your own world, and you
85   might quickly make it right.

DESD: I do not think there is any such woman.

EMILIA: Yes, a dozen, and as many to the vantage as would store the
world they played for.
      But I do think it is their husbands' faults
90   If wives do fall; say that they slack their duties
And pour our treasures into foreign laps,
Or else break out in peevish jealousies,
Throwing restraint upon us, or say they strike us,
Or scant our former having in despite,
95   Why, we have galls, and though we have some grace,
Yet have we some revenge. Let husbands know
Their wives have sense like them; they see and smell
And have their palates both for sweet and sour,
As husbands have. What is it that they do
100   When they change us for others? Is it sport?
I think it is. And doth affection breed it?
I think it doth. Is't frailty that thus errs?
It is so too. And have not we affections,
Desires for sport, and frailty, as men have?
105   Then let them use us well; else let them know,
The ills we do, their ills instruct us so.

DESD: Good night, good night. Heaven me such uses send,
Not to pick bad from bad, but by bad mend!

[Exeunt.]

EMILIA: *The wrong is only a wrong in the world, and if you obtained the world for your deed, it is then a wrong in your own world, one you could quickly make right.*

DESD: *I do not think there is any woman like that.*

EMILIA: *Yes, a dozen, and enough others to populate the world they gambled for. But I think it is the husbands' faults if wives cheat. I think that the men neglect their duties, and pour our treasures into other men's laps. They break out in foolish jealousy, restricting us or striking us. They withhold our allowance out of spite. But we have courage; although we have some grace, we can still have revenge. Husbands should know that their wives have sense like they do; women see and smell and have a taste for both sweet and sour, just as their husbands do. Why do they exchange us for other women? Is it for fun? I think it is. Do they do it because of desire? I think so. Is it because they are weak? I think that as well. Don't women have desires, want to have fun, and are as weak as men? Therefore, men should treat us well, because they should know that the wrongs we do is learned from their wrongs.*

DESD: *Good night, good night. Heaven help me to not follow bad behavior, but to learn from it!*

[Exeunt]

221

ACT V

SCENE 1
Cyprus. A street.

[Enter Iago and Roderigo.]

IAGO: Here, stand behind this bulk; straight will he come:
    Wear thy good rapier bare, and put it home.
    Quick, quick; fear nothing; I'll be at thy elbow.
    It makes us, or it mars us; think on that,
5   And fix most firm thy resolution.

ROD: Be near at hand; I may miscarry in't.

IAGO: Here, at thy hand, be bold, and take thy stand.   *[Retires.]*

ROD: I have no great devotion to the deed;
    And yet he hath given me satisfying reasons:
10   'Tis but a man gone. Forth, my sword; he dies.

IAGO: I have rubb'd this young quat almost to the sense,
    And he grows angry. Now, whether he kill Cassio,
    Or Cassio him, or each do kill the other,
    Every way makes my gain. Live Roderigo,
15   He calls me to a restitution large
    Of gold and jewels that I bobb'd from him,
    As gifts to Desdemona;
    It must not be. If Cassio do remain,
    He hath a daily beauty in his life
20   That makes me ugly; and besides, the Moor

ACT V

SCENE 1
Cyprus. A street.

[Enter Iago and Roderigo]

IAGO: *Here, stand behind this wall. Cassio will be here soon. Keep your sword out, and drive it into your enemy. Quick, quick; do not be afraid. I will be by your side. This will make us or ruin us. Think about that, and resolve to be firm in your purpose.*

ROD: *Stay close by; I may not get it right.*

IAGO: *I'll be here. Be bold, and take your stand.*   [Retires at a distance]

ROD: *I am not committed to this act, yet he has given me good reasons for doing it, it is only one man dead. I'll put my sword forward, and he'll die.*

IAGO: *I have rubbed this young pimple until it is about to pop, and he grows angry. Now, whether he kills Cassio, or Cassio kills him, or they kill each other, I win any way. If Roderigo lives, I have to give back all the jewels that I stole from him to give as gifts to Desdemona. This cannot happen. If Cassio lives, he has a certain beauty in his life that makes me seem ugly; besides, the Moor may reveal my part in this to him. That would put me in a great deal of danger. No, Cassio must die. So be it: I hear him coming.*

May unfold me to him; there stand I in much peril:
No, he must die. Be't so. I hear him coming.

[Enter Cassio.]

ROD: I know his gait; 'tis he. Villain, thou diest!
                              [Makes a pass at Cassio.]

CASSIO: That thrust had been mine enemy indeed,
25   But that my coat is better than thou know'st;
      I will make proof of thine.   *[Draws, and wounds Roderigo.]*

ROD: O, I am slain!
                [Iago from behind wounds Cassio in the leg, and exit.]

CASSIO: I am maim'd forever. Help, ho! Murder! Murder!   *[Falls.]*

[Enter Othello]

OTHELLO: The voice of Cassio; Iago keeps his word.

30   ROD: O, villain that I am!

OTHELLO: It is even so.

CASSIO: O, help, ho! Light! A surgeon!

OTHELLO: 'Tis he. O brave Iago, honest and just,
      That hast such noble sense of thy friend's wrong!
35   Thou teachest me. Minion, your dear lies dead,
      And your unblest fate hies. Strumpet, I come!
      Forth of my heart those charms, thine eyes, are blotted;
      Thy bed luststain'd shall with lust's blood be spotted.   *[Exit.]*

[Enter Lodovico and Gratiano.]

CASSIO: What, ho! No watch? No passage? Murder! Murder!

[Enter Cassio]

ROD: *I know his manner of walking, It is him. Villain, you die!*
                                              [Makes a lunge at Cassio]

CASSIO: *That thrust might have killed me except that my armor is better than you know. I will test yours now.*   [Draws, and wounds Roderigo]

ROD: *Oh, I am killed!*
                    [Iago from behind wounds Cassio in the leg, and exits]

CASSIO: *I am mutilated forever. Help, ho! Murder! Murder!*   [Falls]

[Enter Othello]

OTHELLO: *That is Cassio's voice. Iago has kept his word.*

ROD: *Oh, I am a villain!*

OTHELLO: *That is true.*

CASSIO: *Oh, help, ho! Run! Get a surgeon!*

OTHELLO: *It is he. Oh, brave Iago, honest and just, you understand your friend's trouble nobly! I learn from you. Devil, your dear Cassio lies dead, and your cursed fate is coming. Whore, I am on my way. Your charms and your eyes are erased from my heart. Your lust-stained bed will be stained with your lustful blood.*   [Exit]

[Enter Lodovico and Gratiano]

CASSIO: *What, ho! No guards? No one passing by? Murder! Murder!*

40   Gratiano: 'Tis some mischance; the cry is very direful.

Cassio: O, help!

Lodovico: Hark!

Rod: O wretched villain!

Lodovico: Two or three groan; it is a heavy night:
45   These may be counterfeits; let's think't unsafe
      To come in to the cry without more help.

Rod: Nobody come? Then shall I bleed to death.

Lodovico: Hark!

[Reenter Iago, with a light.]

Gratiano: Here's one comes in his shirt, with light and weapons.

50   Iago: Who's there? Whose noise is this that cries on murder?

Lodovico: We do not know.

Iago: Did not you hear a cry?

Cassio: Here, here! for heaven's sake, help me!

Iago: What's the matter?

55   Gratiano: This is Othello's ancient, as I take it.

Lodovico: The same indeed; a very valiant fellow.

Iago: What are you here that cry so grievously?

Cassio: Iago? O, I am spoil'd, undone by villains!
      Give me some help.

GRATIANO: *There is some disaster. That cry is very desperate.*

CASSIO: *Oh, help!*

LODOVICO: *Listen!*

ROD: *Oh, miserable villain!*

LODOVICO: *Two or three people are groaning. It is a hard night. This may be a trap. Let's assume that it is unsafe to rush in without more help.*

ROD: *Nobody will come? Then I will bleed to death.*

LODOVICO: *Listen!*

[Reenter Iago, with a torch]

GRATIANO: *Here comes a person in armor, with a light and weapons.*

IAGO: *Who's there? Who is making all this noise and calling out "Murder"?*

LODOVICO: *We do not know.*

IAGO: *Did you hear someone cry?*

CASSIO: *Here, here! For heaven's sake, help me!*

IAGO: *What's the matter?*

GRATIANO: *This is Othello's next-in-command, I assume.*

LODOVICO: *Yes it is. He is a very valiant fellow.*

IAGO: *What are you doing here crying so grievously?*

CASSIO: *Iago? Oh, I am injured, ruined by villains! Give me some help.*

60   IAGO: O me, lieutenant! What villains have done this?

      CASSIO: I think that one of them is hereabout,
          And cannot make away.

      IAGO: O treacherous villains!   *[To Lodovico and Gratiano]*
          What are you there? Come in and give some help.

65   ROD: O, help me here!

      CASSIO: That's one of them.

      IAGO: O murderous slave! O villain!   *[Stabs Roderigo.]*

      ROD: O damn'd Iago! O inhuman dog!

      IAGO: Kill men i' the dark! Where be these bloody thieves?
70   How silent is this town! Ho! Murder! Murder!
          What may you be? Are you of good or evil?

      LODOVICO: As you shall prove us, praise us.

      IAGO: Signior Lodovico?

      LODOVICO: He, sir.

75   IAGO: I cry you mercy. Here's Cassio hurt by villains.

      GRATIANO: Cassio?

      IAGO: How is't, brother?

      CASSIO: My leg is cut in two.

      IAGO: Marry, heaven forbid!
80   Light, gentlemen; I'll bind it with my shirt.

IAGO: Oh my, lieutenant! Who has done this?

CASSIO: I think that one of them is around here and can't get away.

IAGO: Oh, treacherous villains! [To Lodovico and Gratiano] What are you doing over there? Come over here and help.

ROD: Oh, help me here!

CASSIO: That's one of them.

IAGO: Oh, murderous slave! Oh, villain!   [He stabs Roderigo]

ROD: Oh, damned Iago! Oh, inhuman dog!

IAGO: You kill men in the dark! Where are these bloodthirsty thieves? This town is silent! Ho! Murder! Murder! [To Lodovico] What are you? Are you friend or enemy?

LODOVICO: As you recognize us, evaluate us.

IAGO: Signior Lodovico?

LODOVICO: I am he, sir.

IAGO: I beg your pardon. Here is Cassio, hurt by villains.

GRATIANO: Cassio!

IAGO: How bad is it, brother?

CASSIO: My leg is cut in half.

IAGO: Heaven forbid! Hold the light, gentlemen; I'll tie the wound with my shirt.

[Enter Bianca.]

BIANCA: What is the matter, ho? Who is't that cried?

IAGO: Who is't that cried!

BIANCA: O my dear Cassio, my sweet Cassio! O Cassio, Cassio, Cassio!

IAGO: O notable strumpet! Cassio, may you suspect
85   Who they should be that have thus mangled you?

CASSIO: No.

GRATIANO: I am sorry to find you thus; I have been to seek you.

IAGO: Lend me a garter. So. O, for a chair,
     To bear him easily hence!

90   BIANCA: Alas, he faints! O Cassio, Cassio, Cassio!

IAGO: Gentlemen all, I do suspect this trash
     To be a party in this injury.
     Patience awhile, good Cassio. Come, come;
     Lend me a light. Know we this face or no?
95   Alas, my friend and my dear countryman
     Roderigo? No—yes, sure. O heaven! Roderigo.

GRATIANO: What, of Venice?

IAGO: Even he, sir. Did you know him?

GRATIANO: Know him! ay.

100   IAGO: Signior Gratiano? I cry you gentle pardon;
     These bloody accidents must excuse my manners,
     That so neglected you.

[Enter Bianca]

BIANCA: *What is the matter? Who cried out?*

IAGO: *Who cried out!*

BIANCA: *Oh, my dear Cassio; my sweet Cassio! Oh, Cassio, Cassio, Cassio!*

IAGO: *Oh, it is the notorious whore! Cassio, do you suspect who injured you?*

CASSIO: *No.*

GRATIANO: *I am sorry to find you like this; I've been looking for you.*

IAGO: *Lend me a belt. There. We need a chair to carry him inside more easily!*

BIANCA: *Alas, he faints! Oh, Cassio, Cassio, Cassio!*

IAGO: *Gentlemen, I suspect this trash played a part in Cassio's injury. Have patience, good Cassio. Come, come; lend me a light. Do we know this face or not? Is this my friend and my dear countryman Roderigo? No—yes, surely. Oh, heaven! Roderigo.*

GRATIANO: *What, Roderigo from Venice?*

IAGO: *That is him, sir. Did you know him?*

GRATIANO: *Know him! Yes.*

IAGO: *Signior Gratiano? I beg your pardon. Excuse my poor manners; this bloody accident has caused me to neglect you.*

GRATIANO: I am glad to see you.

IAGO: How do you, Cassio? O, a chair, a chair!

105   GRATIANO: Roderigo!

IAGO: He, he, 'tis he. *[A chair brought in.]* O, that's well said: the chair.
Some good man bear him carefully from hence;
I'll fetch the general's surgeon.
[To Bianca.] For you, mistress,
110   Save you your labor. He that lies slain here, Cassio,
Was my dear friend; what malice was between you?

CASSIO: None in the world; nor do I know the man.

IAGO: *[To Bianca.]* What, look you pale? O, bear him out o' the air.
                              [Cassio and Roderigo are borne off.]
Stay you, good gentlemen. Look you pale, mistress?
115   Do you perceive the gastness of her eye?
Nay, if you stare, we shall hear more anon.
Behold her well; I pray you, look upon her.
Do you see, gentlemen? Nay, guiltiness will speak,
Though tongues were out of use.

[Enter Emilia.]

120   EMILIA: 'Las, what's the matter? What's the matter, husband?

IAGO: Cassio hath here been set on in the dark
By Roderigo, and fellows that are 'scaped;
He's almost slain, and Roderigo dead.

EMILIA: Alas, good gentleman! alas, good Cassio!

125   IAGO: This is the fruit of whoring. Prithee, Emilia,
Go know of Cassio where he supp'd tonight.
What, do you shake at that?

GRATIANO: I am glad to see you.

IAGO: How are you, Cassio? Oh, a chair, a chair!

GRATIANO: Roderigo!

IAGO: It is he. [A chair is brought in] *Oh, good, the chair. Some good man should carry him carefully from here. I'll get the general's surgeon.* [To Bianca] *As for you, mistress, save your acting. Cassio, the man who lies here dead was my dear friend. What ill-feeling was between you two?*

CASSIO: *None in the world. I don't know him.*

IAGO: [To Bianca] *What, why do you look so pale? Oh, take inside.*
                              [Cassio and Roderigo are carried off]
Good gentlemen, you stay here. Why do you look so pale, mistress? Do you see the terror in her eyes? No, if you look closely, we will hear more before long. Watch her closely, I beg you, watch her. Do you see, gentlemen? Guilt will speak, even without a voice.

[Enter Emilia]

EMILIA: *Alas, what's the matter? What's the matter, husband?*

IAGO: *Cassio has been attacked here in the dark by Roderigo and some other fellows who have escaped. He is almost dead, and Roderigo is dead.*

EMILIA: *Alas, good gentleman! Alas, good Cassio!*

IAGO: *This is what comes from being unfaithful. Emilia, find out where Cassio ate dinner tonight.* [To Bianca] *Why do you shudder at that?*

233

BIANCA: He supp'd at my house; but I therefore shake not.

IAGO: O, did he so? I charge you, go with me.

130 EMILIA: Fie, fie upon thee, strumpet!

BIANCA: I am no strumpet, but of life as honest
    As you that thus abuse me.

EMILIA: As I! foh! fie upon thee!

IAGO: Kind gentlemen, let's go see poor Cassio dress'd.
135   Come, mistress, you must tell's another tale.
    Emilia, run you to the citadel,
    And tell my lord and lady what hath happ'd!
    Will you go on? *[Aside.]* This is the night
    That either makes me or fordoes me quite.

[Exeunt.]

SCENE 2
A bedchamber in the castle.
Desdemona in bed asleep; a light burning.

[Enter Othello.]

OTHELLO: It is the cause, it is the cause, my soul.
    Let me not name it to you, you chaste stars!
    It is the cause. Yet I'll not shed her blood,
    Nor scar that whiter skin of hers than snow
5   And smooth as monumental alabaster.
    Yet she must die, else she'll betray more men.
    Put out the light, and then put out the light.
    If I quench thee, thou flaming minister,
    I can again thy former light restore,

BIANCA: *He ate at my house, but I am not shaking about that.*

IAGO: *Oh, he did? I order you to come with me.*

EMILIA: *To hell with you, whore!*

BIANCA: *I am no whore. I live as honest a life as you who are abusing me.*

EMILIA: *As honest as I am! Shame on you!*

IAGO: *Kind gentlemen, let's go see that poor Cassio's wounds are dressed. Come, mistress, you must tell us some more lies. Emilia, run to the castle and tell my lord and lady what has happened. I ask you, will you go? [Aside] This is the night that either makes me or does me in.*

[Exeunt]

SCENE 2
In a bed chamber in the castle,
Desdemona is in bed asleep; a candle is burning.

[Enter Othello]

OTHELLO: *It is the cause, the cause, my soul. I won't say the word to you, you pure stars!—It is the cause. But I will not shed her blood, or scar that skin of hers that is whiter than snow, and smooth as the marble used for making tombs. Yet she must die, or else she will betray more men. Put out the candle: and then put out her light. If I smother your light, you burning servant, I can restore your former light, if I change my mind. But once I put out Desdemona's light, her cunning pattern of natural perfection, I do not know of any type of divine heat that can re-light it. When I have plucked your rose, I cannot make it grow again. It must wither. I'll smell it on the tree.*

10   Should I repent me; but once put out thy light,
        Thou cunning'st pattern of excelling nature,
        I know not where is that Promethean heat
        That can thy light relume. When I have pluck'd the rose,
        I cannot give it vital growth again,
15   It must needs wither; I'll smell it on the tree. *[Kisses her.]*
        O, balmy breath, that dost almost persuade
        Justice to break her sword! One more, one more;
        Be thus when thou art dead, and I will kill thee,
        And love thee after. One more, and this the last:
20   So sweet was ne'er so fatal. I must weep,
        But they are cruel tears; this sorrow's heavenly,
        It strikes where it doth love. She wakes.

        DESD: Who's there? Othello?

        OTHELLO: Ay, Desdemona.

25   DESD: Will you come to bed, my lord?

        OTHELLO: Have you pray'd tonight, Desdemona?

        DESD: Ay, my lord.

        OTHELLO: If you bethink yourself of any crime
                Unreconciled as yet to heaven and grace,
30   Solicit for it straight.

        DESD: Alas, my lord, what may you mean by that?

        OTHELLO: Well, do it, and be brief; I will walk by:
                I would not kill thy unprepared spirit;
                No, heaven forfend! I would not kill thy soul.

35   DESD: Talk you of killing?

        OTHELLO: Ay, I do.

236

[Kissing her] *Ah warm, gentle breath, that almost persuades Justice to break her sword. One more kiss, one more kiss. If you are this beautiful when you are dead, I will kill you, and still love you after. One more kiss, and this is the last. Something so sweet has never been this fatal. I must cry, but they are cruel tears. This is a sacred sorrow. It hits where it loves. She is waking up.*

DESD: *Who's there? Othello?*

OTHELLO: *Yes. Desdemona.*

DESD: *Will you come to bed, my lord?*

OTHELLO: *Have you prayed tonight, Desdemona?*

DESD: *Yes, my lord.*

OTHELLO: *If you think you are guilty of any crime which you have not yet confessed, ask for forgiveness right now.*

DESD: *Alas, my lord, what do you mean by that?*

OTHELLO: *Well, do it, and be quick about it. I will walk back here. I would not kill your unprepared soul. No, heaven forbid! I would not kill your soul.*

DESD: *Are you talking about killing?*

OTHELLO: *Yes, I am.*

DESD: Then heaven have mercy on me!

OTHELLO: Amen, with all my heart!

DESD: If you say so, I hope you will not kill me.

40 OTHELLO: Hum!

DESD: And yet I fear you, for you are fatal then
   When your eyes roll so. Why I should fear I know not,
   Since guiltiness I know not; but yet I feel I fear.

OTHELLO: Think on thy sins.

45 DESD: They are loves I bear to you.

OTHELLO: Ay, and for that thou diest.

DESD: That death's unnatural that kills for loving.
   Alas, why gnaw you so your nether lip?
   Some bloody passion shakes your very frame:
50 These are portents; but yet I hope, I hope,
   They do not point on me.

OTHELLO: Peace, and be still!

DESD: I will so. What's the matter?

OTHELLO: That handkerchief which I so loved and gave thee
55 Thou gavest to Cassio.

DESD: No, by my life and soul!
   Send for the man, and ask him.

OTHELLO: Sweet soul, take heed,
   Take heed of perjury; thou are on thy deathbed.

DESD: *Then heaven have mercy on me!*

OTHELLO: *Amen, with all my heart!*

DESD: *If you say so, I hope you will not kill me.*

OTHELLO: *Hum!*

DESD: *I fear you. You are deadly when your eyes roll like that. I don't know why I should fear you, since I am not guilty of anything, but I am still afraid.*

OTHELLO: *Think about your sins.*

DESD: *My only sin is the love I have for you.*

OTHELLO: *Yes, and for that you will die.*

DESD: *Death is unnatural when the killing is done for love. Alas, why are you chewing on your bottom lip like that? Some bloody anger shakes your whole body. These are bad signs, but I still hope, I hope, they are not against me.*

OTHELLO: *Peace, and be still!*

DESD: *I will. What's the matter?*

OTHELLO: *That handkerchief that I loved so much and gave to you, you gave to Cassio.*

DESD: *No, I swear on my life and soul! Send for him, and ask him.*

OTHELLO: *Sweet soul, be careful; please consider the sin of lying. You are on your deathbed.*

60   DESD: Ay, but not yet to die.

OTHELLO: Yes, presently:
     Therefore confess thee freely of thy sin;
     For to deny each article with oath
     Cannot remove nor choke the strong conception
65   That I do groan withal. Thou art to die.

DESD: Then Lord have mercy on me!

OTHELLO: I say, amen.

DESD: And have you mercy too! I never did
     Offend you in my life; never loved Cassio
70   But with such general warranty of heaven
     As I might love. I never gave him token.

OTHELLO: By heaven, I saw my handkerchief in 's hand.
     O perjured woman! Thou dost stone my heart,
     And makest me call what I intend to do
75   A murder, which I thought a sacrifice:
     I saw the handkerchief.

DESD: He found it then;
     I never gave it him. Send for him hither;
     Let him confess a truth.

80   OTHELLO: He hath confess'd.

DESD: What, my lord?

OTHELLO: That he hath used thee.

DESD: How? unlawfully?

OTHELLO: Ay.

DESD: *Yes, but I am not yet dead.*

OTHELLO: *Yes, but soon. Therefore, confess your sin freely. To deny each thing by swearing against it cannot change the strong resolve that I have within me. You are going to die.*

DESD: *Then Lord have mercy on me!*

OTHELLO: *I say, amen.*

DESD: *And have mercy on you too! I never wronged you in my life. I never loved Cassio, except for the kind of love heaven tells us to have. I never gave him a gift.*

OTHELLO: *I swear, I saw my handkerchief in his hand. Oh, lying woman! You turn my heart to stone and make me call this deed I am about to commit, a murder, which I thought was a sacrifice. I saw the handkerchief.*

DESD: *He found it then. I never gave it him. Send for him. Let him confess the truth.*

OTHELLO: *He has confessed.*

DESD: *What, my lord?*

OTHELLO: *That he has used you.*

DESD: *How? Unlawfully?*

OTHELLO: *Yes.*

85   DESD: He will not say so.

OTHELLO: No, his mouth is stopp'd;
    Honest Iago hath ta'en order for't.

DESD: O, my fear interprets! What, is he dead?

OTHELLO: Had all his hairs been lives, my great revenge
90   Had stomach for them all.

DESD: Alas, he is betray'd, and I undone!

OTHELLO: Out, strumpet! Weep'st thou for him to my face?

DESD: O, banish me, my lord, but kill me not!

OTHELLO: Down, strumpet!

95   DESD: Kill me tomorrow; let me live tonight!

OTHELLO: Nay, if you strive—

DESD: But half an hour!

OTHELLO: Being done, there is no pause.

DESD: But while I say one prayer!

100 OTHELLO: It is too late. [He stifles her.]

EMILIA: [Within.] My lord, my lord! What, ho! my lord, my lord!

OTHELLO: What noise is this? Not dead? not yet quite dead?
    I that am cruel am yet merciful;
    I would not have thee linger in thy pain. So, so.

105 EMILIA: [Within.] What, ho! my lord, my lord!

DESD: *He would not say that.*

OTHELLO: *No, his mouth has been stopped. Honest Iago has taken care of it.*

DESD: *Oh! My fear guesses at it. What, is Cassio dead?*

OTHELLO: *If all his hairs had been alive, my revenge had stomach enough to kill all of them.*

DESD: *Alas! He is betrayed, and I am condemned.*

OTHELLO: *Out, whore! Do you cry for him to my face?*

DESD: *Oh, banish me, my lord, but don't kill me!*

OTHELLO: *Sit down, whore!*

DESD: *Kill me tomorrow. Let me live tonight!*

OTHELLO: *No, if you resist—*

DESD: *For just half an hour!*

OTHELLO: *Now that I have started, I will not stop.*

DESD: *But let me say one prayer!*

OTHELLO: *It is too late.* [He suffocates her]

EMILIA: [Within] *My lord, my lord! What, ho! My lord, my lord!*

OTHELLO: *What is that noise? Not dead? Not quite dead yet? Although I am cruel, I am also merciful. I will not have you linger in pain. So, so.* [Finishes job]

EMILIA: [Within] *What, ho! My lord, my lord!*

OTHELLO: Who's there?

EMILIA: [Within.] O, good my lord, I would speak a word with you!

OTHELLO: Yes, 'tis Emilia. By and by. She's dead.
    'Tis like she comes to speak of Cassio's death.
110   The noise was here. Ha! no more moving?
    Still as the grave. Shall she come in? were't good?
    I think she stirs again. No. What's best to do?
    If she come in, she'll sure speak to my wife.
    My wife! My wife! What wife? I have no wife.
115   O, insupportable! O heavy hour!
    Methinks it should be now a huge eclipse
    Of sun and moon, and that the affrighted globe
    Should yawn at alteration.

EMILIA: [Within.] I do beseech you
120   That I may speak with you, O, good my lord!

OTHELLO: I had forgot thee. O, come in, Emilia.
    Soft, by and by. Let me the curtains draw.
    Where art thou?   [Unlocks the door.]

[Enter Emilia.]
    What's the matter with thee now?

125 EMILIA: O, my good lord, yonder's foul murders done!

OTHELLO: What, now?

EMILIA: But now, my lord.

OTHELLO: It is the very error of the moon;
    She comes more nearer earth than she was wont
130   And makes men mad.

EMILIA: Cassio, my lord, hath kill'd a young Venetian
    Call'd Roderigo:

244

OTHELLO: *Who is there?*

EMILIA: [Within] *Oh, good my lord, I need to speak with you!*

OTHELLO: *Yes, it is Emilia. Just a minute. She's dead. Emilia probably comes to report Cassio's death. The noise came from here. Ha! No more moving? Still as the grave. Should she come in? Is it okay? I think she stirs again. No. What's best to do? If she comes in, she will want to speak to my wife. My wife! My wife! What wife? I have no wife. Oh, intolerable! Oh, terrible hour! I think there should be now a huge eclipse of sun and moon, and the entire world will feel this drastic change.*

EMILIA: [Within] *I beg you. I need to speak with you, Oh, good my lord!*

OTHELLO: *I had forgotten about you. Oh, come in, Emilia. Be quiet. Let me close the curtains. Where are you?* [Unlocks the door]

[Enter Emilia]
What's the matter with you now?

EMILIA: *Oh, my good lord, foul murders have been committed outside!*

OTHELLO: *When? Now?*

EMILIA: *Just now, my lord.*

OTHELLO: *The problem is the moon. She has come closer to the earth than she should, and that makes men crazy.*

EMILIA: *Cassio, my lord, has killed a young Venetian called Roderigo.*

OTHELLO: Roderigo kill'd?
   And Cassio kill'd?

135 EMILIA: No, Cassio is not kill'd.

OTHELLO: Not Cassio kill'd! Then murder 's out of tune,
   And sweet revenge grows harsh.

DESD: O, falsely, falsely murdered!

EMILIA: Alas, what cry is that?

140 OTHELLO: That? what?

EMILIA: Out, and alas! That was my lady's voice.
   Help! help, ho! help! O lady, speak again!
   Sweet Desdemona! O sweet mistress, speak!

DESD: A guiltless death I die.

145 EMILIA: O, who hath done this deed?

DESD: Nobody; I myself. Farewell;
   Commend me to my kind lord. O, farewell!   [Dies.]

OTHELLO: Why, how should she be murdered?

EMILIA: Alas, who knows?

150 OTHELLO: You heard her say herself, it was not I.

EMILIA: She said so; I must needs report the truth.

OTHELLO: She's like a liar gone to burning hell;
   'Twas I that kill'd her.

EMILIA: O, the more angel she,
155   And you the blacker devil!

246

OTHELLO: *Roderigo is killed? And Cassio is killed?*

EMILIA: *No, Cassio is not killed.*

OTHELLO: *Cassio has not been killed! Then murder is not doing its job, and sweet revenge has grown sour.*

DESD: *Oh, falsely, falsely murdered!*

EMILIA: *Alas, who is making that noise?*

OTHELLO: *That! What?*

EMILIA: *Out, and alas! That was my lady's voice. Help! Help, ho! Help! Oh, lady, speak again! Sweet Desdemona! Oh, sweet mistress, speak!*

DESD: *I die a guiltless death.*

EMILIA: *Oh, who has done this deed?*

DESD: *Nobody. I did it myself. Farewell. Remember me to my kind lord. Oh, farewell!*   [Dies]

OTHELLO: *Why? How was she be murdered?*

EMILIA: *Alas, who knows?*

OTHELLO: *You heard her say herself that it was not I.*

EMILIA: *She said so. I must tell the truth.*

OTHELLO: *She is a liar and will burn in hell. It was I who killed her.*

EMILIA: *Oh, that makes her more of an angel, and makes you a blacker devil!*

OTHELLO: She turn'd to folly, and she was a whore.

EMILIA: Thou dost belie her, and thou art a devil.

OTHELLO: She was false as water.

EMILIA: Thou art rash as fire, to say
160   That she was false. O, she was heavenly true!

OTHELLO: Cassio did top her; ask thy husband else.
    O, I were damn'd beneath all depth in hell,
    But that I did proceed upon just grounds
    To this extremity. Thy husband knew it all.

165 EMILIA: My husband!

OTHELLO: Thy husband.

EMILIA: That she was false to wedlock?

OTHELLO: Ay, with Cassio. Nay, had she been true,
    If heaven would make me such another world
170   Of one entire and perfect chrysolite,
    I'ld not have sold her for it.

EMILIA: My husband!

OTHELLO: Ay, 'twas he that told me first:
    An honest man he is, and hates the slime
175   That sticks on filthy deeds.

EMILIA: My husband?

OTHELLO: What needs this iteration, woman? I say thy husband.

EMILIA: O mistress, villainy hath made mocks with love!
    My husband say that she was false!

OTHELLO: *She turned to cheating on me, and she was a whore.*

EMILIA: *You are lying about her, and you are a devil.*

OTHELLO: *She was as unfaithful as water.*

EMILIA: *You are as hasty as fire to say that she was unfaithful. Oh, she was heavenly true!*

OTHELLO: *Cassio had sex with her. Ask your husband. Oh, I would be damned deep in the depths of hell, but I acted out of just reasons to do this extreme act. Your husband knew everything.*

EMILIA: *My husband!*

OTHELLO: *Your husband.*

EMILIA: *He said Desdemona was false to your marriage?*

OTHELLO: *Yes, with Cassio. Now, if she had been true, if heaven would make me another world of one entire and perfect precious stone, I would not have sold her for it.*

EMILIA: *My husband!*

OTHELLO: *Yes, he first told me about it. Being as honest as he is, he hates the slime that sticks on filthy deeds.*

EMILIA: *My husband?*

OTHELLO: *Why do you keep repeating that, woman? I said your husband.*

EMILIA: *Oh, mistress, treachery has made a joke of love. My husband says that she was unfaithful!*

180 OTHELLO: He, woman;
      I say thy husband. Dost understand the word?
      My friend, thy husband, honest, honest Iago.

EMILIA: If he say so, may his pernicious soul
      Rot half a grain a day! He lies to the heart.
185   She was too fond of her most filthy bargain.

OTHELLO: Ha!

EMILIA: Do thy worst;
      This deed of thine is no more worthy heaven
      Than thou wast worthy her.

190 OTHELLO: Peace, you were best.

EMILIA: Thou hast not half that power to do me harm
      As I have to be hurt. O gull! O dolt!
      As ignorant as dirt! Thou hast done a deed—
      I care not for thy sword; I'll make thee known,
195   Though I lost twenty lives. Help! help, ho! help!
      The Moor hath kill'd my mistress! Murder, murder!

[Enter Montano, Gratiano, Iago, and others.]

MONTANO: What is the matter? How now, general?

EMILIA: O, are you come, Iago? You have done well,
      That men must lay their murders on your neck.

200 GRATIANO: What is the matter?

EMILIA: Disprove this villain, if thou be'st a man:
      He says thou told'st him that his wife was false;
      I know thou didst not, thou'rt not such a villain.
      Speak, for my heart is full.

OTHELLO: *Your husband, woman. I said your husband. Do you understand the word? My friend, your husband, honest, honest Iago.*

EMILIA: *If he say so, may his evil soul slowly rot, a tiny bit each day! He is lying to the heart. She was too passionate of her marriage to you.*

OTHELLO: *Ha!*

EMILIA: *Say your worst. This deed of yours is no more worthy of heaven than you were worthy of her.*

OTHELLO: *Keep quiet; do yourself a favor.*

EMILIA: *You do not have the power to hurt me more than I have already been hurt. Oh, fool! Oh, idiot! You are as ignorant as dirt! You have done a deed—I don't care about your sword. I will expose you, even if it costs me twenty lives. Help! help, ho! help! The Moor has killed my mistress! Murder! Murder!*

[Enter Montano, Gratiano, Iago, and others]

MONTANO: *What is the matter? What's happening here, general?*

EMILIA: *Oh, are you here, Iago? You have done so well that men blame you for the murders they commit.*

GRATIANO: *What is the matter?*

EMILIA: *Prove this villain wrong, if you are a man. He says that you told him that his wife was unfaithful. I know you did not, for you are not such a villain. Speak, because my heart is full of sorrow.*

205 IAGO: I told him what I thought, and told no more
       Than what he found himself was apt and true.

EMILIA: But did you ever tell him she was false?

IAGO: I did.

EMILIA: You told a lie, an odious, damned lie;
210   Upon my soul, a lie, a wicked lie!
       She false with Cassio? Did you say with Cassio?

IAGO: With Cassio, mistress. Go to, charm your tongue.

EMILIA: I will not charm my tongue; I am bound to speak.
       My mistress here lies murdered in her bed

215 ALL: O heavens forfend!

EMILIA: And your reports have set the murder on.

OTHELLO: Nay, stare not, masters; it is true indeed.

GRATIANO: 'Tis a strange truth.

MONTANO: O monstrous act!

220 EMILIA: Villainy, villainy, villainy!
       I think upon't, I think, I smell't, O villainy!
       I thought so then. I'll kill myself for grief:
       O villainy, villainy!

IAGO: What, are you mad? I charge you, get you home.

225 EMILIA: Good gentlemen, let me have leave to speak;
       'Tis proper I obey him, but not now.
       Perchance, Iago, I will ne'er go home.

IAGO: *I told him what I thought, and I told no more than what he thought was likely and true.*

EMILIA: *But did you ever tell him she was unfaithful?*

IAGO: *I did.*

EMILIA: *You told a lie, a hateful, damned lie. I swear upon my soul—a lie, a wicked lie! She—having an affair with Cassio? Did you say with Cassio?*

IAGO: *With Cassio, mistress. Now, get out, and control your mouth.*

EMILIA: *I will not hold my tongue. I must speak. My mistress lies murdered here in her bed.*

ALL: *Oh, heaven forbid!*

EMILIA: *And your gossip is what led to the murder.*

OTHELLO: *No, don't stare, gentlemen; it is true, positively.*

GRATIANO: *It is a shocking truth.*

MONTANO: *Oh, monstrous act!*

EMILIA: *Villainy, villainy, villainy! I think about it— I think. I smell it. Oh, villainy! I thought so then. I'll kill myself out of grief. Oh, villainy, villainy!*

IAGO: *What, have you gone crazy? I order you to get yourself home.*

EMILIA: *Good gentlemen, let me have your permission to speak. It is proper that I obey him, but not now. Maybe, Iago, I will never go home.*

OTHELLO: O! O! O!   *[Falls on the bed.]*

EMILIA: Nay, lay thee down and roar;
230   For thou hast kill'd the sweetest innocent
    That e'er did lift up eye.

OTHELLO: *[Rises.]* O, she was foul!
    I scarce did know you, uncle; there lies your niece,
    Whose breath indeed these hands have newly stopp'd.
235   I know this act shows horrible and grim.

GRATIANO: Poor Desdemon! I am glad thy father's dead:
    Thy match was mortal to him, and pure grief
    Shore his old thread in twain; did he live now,
    This sight would make him do a desperate turn,
240   Yea, curse his better angel from his side,
    And fall to reprobation.

OTHELLO: 'Tis pitiful, but yet Iago knows
    That she with Cassio hath the act of shame
    A thousand times committed. Cassio confess'd it,
245   And she did gratify his amorous works
    With that recognizance and pledge of love
    Which I first gave her. I saw it in his hand:
    It was a handkerchief, an antique token
    My father gave my mother.

250 EMILIA: O heaven! O heavenly powers!

IAGO: 'Zounds! Hold your peace.

EMILIA: 'Twill out, 'twill. I peace!
    No, I will speak as liberal as the north;
    Let heaven and men and devils, let them all,
255   All, all, cry shame against me, yet I'll speak.

IAGO: Be wise, and get you home.

OTHELLO: *Oh! Oh! Oh!* [He falls on the bed]

EMILIA: *Lay yourself down and roar. For you have killed the sweetest, most innocent woman that ever looked up to heaven.*

OTHELLO: [Rising] *Oh, she was unfaithful! I hardly knew you, uncle. Your niece lies dead there; these hands have just stopped her breath. I know this act looks horrible and grim.*

GRATIANO: *Poor Desdemona! I am glad your father is dead. Your marriage killed him. Pure grief cut his life short. If he were alive now, this sight would have made him damn the angel on his side and fall to thoughts of sin.*

OTHELLO: *It is pitiful, but still Iago knows that she committed thousands of shameful acts with Cassio. Cassio confessed it. And she indulged his love by giving him that souvenir, that token of love, the first gift I ever gave her. I saw it in his hand. It was a handkerchief, an antique gift that my father gave to my mother.*

EMILIA: *Oh heaven! Oh, heavenly powers!*

IAGO: *Come now, be quiet.*

EMILIA: *The truth will come out. It will come out. Be quiet! No, I will speak as freely as the violent north wind. Let heaven and men and devil—let them all, all, all, cry that I am wrong, but I will speak.*

IAGO: *Be wise, and get yourself home.*

255

EMILIA: I will not.

[Iago offers to stab Emilia.]

GRATIANO: Fie! Your sword upon a woman?

EMILIA: O thou dull Moor! That handkerchief thou speak'st of
260   I found by fortune and did give my husband;
For often with a solemn earnestness,
More than indeed belong'd to such a trifle,
He begg'd of me to steal it.

IAGO: Villainous whore!

265   EMILIA: She give it Cassio? No, alas, I found it,
And I did give't my husband.

IAGO: Filth, thou liest!

EMILIA: By heaven, I do not, I do not, gentlemen.
O murderous coxcomb! What should such a fool
270   Do with so good a wife?

OTHELLO: Are there not stones in heaven
But what serve for thunder? Precious villain!
[He runs at Iago, but Montano disarms him.]
[Iago stabs Emilia and exits.]

GRATIANO: The woman falls; sure, he hath kill'd his wife.

275   EMILIA: Ay, ay! O, lay me by my mistress' side.

GRATIANO: He's gone, but his wife's kill'd.

MONTANO: 'Tis a notorious villain. Take you this weapon,
Which I have here recover'd from the Moor:
Come, guard the door without; let him not pass,
280   But kill him rather. I'll after that same villain,
For 'tis a damned slave.   *[Exeunt all but Othello and Emilia].*

EMILIA: *I will not.*

[Iago draws his sword to stab Emilia]

GRATIANO: *Fie! Draw your sword upon a woman?*

EMILIA: *Oh, you stupid Moor! I happened to find that handkerchief that you speak of and gave it to my husband He often mentioned the item and begged me to steal it.*

IAGO: *Villainous whore!*

EMILIA: *Desdemona gave it to Cassio? No, alas! I found it, and I gave it my husband.*

IAGO: *Filth, you are lying!*

EMILIA: *I swear by heaven, I am not. I am not lying, gentlemen. Oh, murderous fool! What was such a fool doing with such a good woman?*

OTHELLO: *Do the stones in heaven make only thunder? Worthless villain!*
[He runs at Iago but Montano takes his sword. Iago stabs Emilia and exits]

GRATIANO: *The woman falls. He has killed his wife.*

EMILIA: *Yes, yes. Oh, lay me by my mistress' side.*

GRATIANO: *He's gone, and his wife has been killed.*

MONTANO: *He is a notorious villain. Take this weapon which I have removed from the Moor. Come, go outside and guard the door. Do not let Othello out; kill him if you must. I will go after that villain Iago; he is a damned slave.*
[Exit all but Othello and Emilia]

OTHELLO: I am not valiant neither,
 But every puny whipster gets my sword.
 But why should honor outlive honesty?
285 Let it go all.

EMILIA: What did thy song bode, lady?
 Hark, canst thou hear me? I will play the swan,
 And die in music.
  [Sings.] "Willow, willow, willow."
290 Moor, she was chaste; she loved thee, cruel Moor;
 So come my soul to bliss, as I speak true;
 So speaking as I think, I die, I die. [Dies.]

OTHELLO: I have another weapon in this chamber;
 O, here it is. Uncle, I must come forth.

295 GRATIANO: [Within.] If thou attempt it, it will cost thee dear:
 Thou hast no weapon, and perforce must suffer.

OTHELLO: Look in upon me then, and speak with me,
 Or, naked as I am, I will assault thee.

[Reenter Gratiano.]

GRATIANO: What is the matter?

300 OTHELLO: Behold, I have a weapon;
 A better never did itself sustain
 Upon a soldier's thigh. I have seen the day
 That with this little arm and this good sword
 I have made my way through more impediments
305 Than twenty times your stop. But, O vain boast!
 Who can control his fate? 'Tis not so now.
 Be not afraid, though you do see me weapon'd;
 Here is my journey's end, here is my butt
 And very seamark of my utmost sail.
310 Do you go back dismay'd? 'Tis a lost fear:

OTHELLO: *I am not brave either. I've let a puny little boy get my sword. But why should honor outlive honesty? Let it all go.*

EMILIA: *What did your song foretell, lady? Listen, can't you hear me? I will be like a swan and die in music.*
          [Singing] *"Willow, willow, willow,"*
—*Moor, she was pure; she loved you, cruel Moor. May my soul go peacefully to heaven because I am speaking the truth. And, saying what I think, I die, I die.* [Dies]

OTHELLO: *I have another weapon in this room. It is a Spanish sword, hardened in cold water. Uncle, I must get out.*

GRATIANO: [Within] *If you attempt it, it will cost you dearly. You have no weapon, and, therefore, you must suffer.*

OTHELLO: *Look in on me then and speak with me, or, unarmed as I am, I will attack you.*

[Reenter Gratiano]

GRATIANO: *What is the matter?*

OTHELLO: *See, I have a weapon. No better sword ever rested upon a soldier's thigh. I recall the days when, with this sword in my hand, I cut through many obstacles without stopping. But, Oh, vain boast! Who can control his fate? It is not so now. I will not hurt you. Don't be afraid, even though you see me with a weapon. Here is my journey's end; here is my bottom. The sea has marked my last sail. Do you step back dismayed? It is a wasted fear. You can use even a weak weed against Othello's breast, and he will fall. Where should Othello go? Now, how do you look now? Oh, ill-fated wench! Pale as your nightgown! When we shall meet at Judgement Day, this look of yours will hurl my soul from heaven, and devils will snatch at it. Cold, cold, my girl! Just like your innocence. Oh, cursed villain! Whip me, you devils of*

Man but a rush against Othello's breast,
And he retires. Where should Othello go?
Now, how dost thou look now? O illstarr'd wench!
Pale as thy smock! When we shall meet at compt,
315   This look of thine will hurl my soul from heaven,
And fiends will snatch at it. Cold, cold, my girl
Even like thy chastity. O cursed, cursed slave!
Whip me, ye devils,
From the possession of this heavenly sight!
320   Blow me about in winds! Roast me in sulphur!
Wash me in steepdown gulfs of liquid fire!
O Desdemon! dead, Desdemon! dead!
O! O! O!

[Enter Lodovico, Montano, Cassio carried in a chair, and Officers with Iago, prisoner.]

LODOVICO: Where is this rash and most unfortunate man?

325 OTHELLO: That's he that was Othello. Here I am.

LODOVICO: Where is that viper? Bring the villain forth.

OTHELLO: I look down towards his feet; but that's a fable.
    If that thou be'st a devil, I cannot kill thee.   *[Wounds Iago.]*

LODOVICO: Wrench his sword from him.

330 IAGO: I bleed, sir, but not kill'd.

OTHELLO: I am not sorry neither. I'ld have thee live,
    For, in my sense, 'tis happiness to die.

LODOVICO: O thou Othello, that wert once so good,
    What shall be said to thee?

this heavenly sight! Blow me about in winds! Roast me in fire! Wash me in gulfs of lava! Oh, Desdemona! Desdemona! Dead! Oh! Oh! Oh!

[Enter Lodovico. Montano; Cassio is carried in a chair, and guards accompany Iago, the prisoner]

LODOVICO: *Where is this rash and most unfortunate man?*

OTHELLO: *That man was Othello. Here I am.*

LODOVICO: [Looking for Iago] *Where is that snake? Bring the villain forward.*

OTHELLO: *I look down towards his feet to see his cloven hoofs of a devil; but that's a fable. If you are a devil, I cannot kill you.* [Othello stabs and wounds Iago]

LODOVICO: *Pull the sword from him.*

IAGO: *I bleed, sir, but I am not killed.*

OTHELLO: *I am not sorry you live; I would like you to live. The way I see it, happiness would be to die.*

LODOVICO: *Oh, Othello, you who were once so good, what will be said about you?*

335 OTHELLO: Why, anything;
      An honorable murderer, if you will,
      For nought did I in hate, but all in honor.

    LODOVICO: This wretch hath part confess'd his villainy.
      Did you and he consent in Cassio's death?

340 OTHELLO: Ay.

    CASSIO: Dear general, I never gave you cause.

    OTHELLO: I do believe it, and I ask your pardon.
      Will you, I pray, demand that demidevil
      Why he hath thus ensnared my soul and body?

345 IAGO: Demand me nothing; what you know: you know.
      From this time forth I never will speak word.

    LODOVICO: What, not to pray?

    GRATIANO: Torments will ope your lips.

    OTHELLO: Well, thou dost best.

350 LODOVICO: Sir, you shall understand what hath befall'n,
      Which, as I think, you know not. Here is a letter
      Found in the pocket of the slain Roderigo,
      And here another. The one of them imports
      The death of Cassio to be undertook
355   By Roderigo.

    OTHELLO: O villain!

    CASSIO: Most heathenish and most gross!

    LODOVICO: Now here's another discontented paper,

OTHELLO: *Why, anything. You can call me an honorable murderer. Because I did nothing out of hate. I did everything for honor.*

LODOVICO: *This wretch has confessed part of his villainy. Did you and Iago conspire to kill Cassio?*

OTHELLO: *Yes.*

CASSIO: *Dear general, I never gave you a reason to kill me.*

OTHELLO: *I believe you, and I ask for your forgiveness. Will you, I beg you, demand that half-devil to explain he has trapped my soul and body like this?*

IAGO: [Defiantly] *Demand nothing of me. What you know, you know. From this moment on, I will never speak again.*

LODOVICO: *What, not even to pray?*

GRATIANO: *Torture will make you talk.*

OTHELLO: *Well, do your best.*

LODOVICO: *Sir, you will understand what has happened, which I don't think you are aware of. Here is a letter found in the pocket of the dead Roderigo. And here is another letter. This one tells how Cassio is to be killed by Roderigo.*

OTHELLO: *Oh, villain!*

CASSIO: *Most unholy and most evil!*

LODOVICO: *Now here's another sad letter, also found in his pocket. This, it*

Found in his pocket too; and this, it seems,
360   Roderigo meant to have sent this damned villain;
But that, belike, Iago in the interim
Came in and satisfied him.

OTHELLO: O the pernicious caitiff!
How came you, Cassio, by that handkerchief
365   That was my wife's?

CASSIO: I found it in my chamber;
And he himself confess'd but even now
That there he dropp'd it for a special purpose
Which wrought to his desire.

370 OTHELLO: O fool! fool! fool!

CASSIO: There is besides in Roderigo's letter,
How he upbraids Iago, that he made him
Brave me upon the watch, whereon it came
That I was cast. And even but now he spake
375   After long seeming dead, Iago hurt him,
Iago set him on.

LODOVICO: You must forsake this room, and go with us:
Your power and your command is taken off,
And Cassio rules in Cyprus. For this slave,
380   If there be any cunning cruelty
That can torment him much and hold him long,
It shall be his. You shall close prisoner rest,
Till that the nature of your fault be known
To the Venetian state. Come, bring away.

385 OTHELLO: Soft you; a word or two before you go.
I have done the state some service, and they know't.
No more of that. I pray you, in your letters,
When you shall these unlucky deeds relate,
Speak of me as I am; nothing extenuate,

seems, Roderigo meant to send to this damned villain, but before it was sent, Iago came in and killed him.

OTHELLO: Oh, the evil coward! How did you get my wife's handkerchief, Cassio?

CASSIO: I found it in my chamber. And Iago himself confessed just now that he dropped it there as part of his plan.

OTHELLO: Oh, fool! fool! fool!

CASSIO: There is more in Roderigo's letter. He scolds Iago for making him attack me when I was on the watch, the one when I lost my position. Even though he is dead, Roderigo still speaks through the letter about how Iago hurt him and urged him on.

LODOVICO: You must leave this room, and come with us. Your power and your command has been taken from you, and Cassio rules in Cyprus. As for this scoundrel Iago, if there are any tortures to torment him severely and for a long time, he will receive them. Othello, you will remain a prisoner until the nature of your action is reported to the Venetian state. Come, take them away.

OTHELLO: Please, a word or two before you go. I have served this state, and they know it. No more about that. I beg you, in your letters, when you tell about these disastrous events, speak of me as I am. Do not minimize it, or add to it out of hatred. Then you will be describing someone who did not love wisely, but who loved too well. A person not easily made jealous, but when

390   Nor set down aught in malice. Then must you speak
          Of one that loved not wisely but too well;
          Of one not easily jealous, but, being wrought,
          Perplex'd in the extreme; of one whose hand,
          Like the base Indian, threw a pearl away

395   Richer than all his tribe; of one whose subdued eyes,
          Albeit unused to the melting mood,
          Drop tears as fast as the Arabian trees
          Their medicinal gum. Set you down this;
          And say besides, that in Aleppo once,

400   Where a malignant and a turban'd Turk
          Beat a Venetian and traduced the state,
          I took by the throat the circumcised dog
          And smote him, thus.   *[Stabs himself.]*

LODOVICO: O bloody period!

405 GRATIANO: All that's spoke is marr'd.

OTHELLO: I kiss'd thee ere I kill'd thee. No way but this, Killing
          myself, to die upon a kiss.   *[Falls on the bed, and dies.]*

CASSIO: This did I fear, but thought he had no weapon;
          For he was great of heart.

410 LODOVICO: *[To Iago.]* O Spartan dog,
          More fell than anguish, hunger, or the sea!
          Look on the tragic loading of this bed;
          This is thy work. The object poisons sight;
          Let it be hid. Gratiano, keep the house,

415   And seize upon the fortunes of the Moor,
          For they succeed on you. To you, Lord Governor,
          Remains the censure of this hellish villain,
          The time, the place, the torture. O, enforce it!
          Myself will straight aboard, and to the state

420   This heavy act with heavy heart relate.
                         [Exeunt.]

jealous became extremely disturbed. A person whose hand, like the corrupt Judas, threw a pearl richer than all his tribe away. A person whose overwhelmed eyes, not used to being in despair, dropped tears as fast as the Arabian trees drop their medicinal sap. Write that down, and also say, that in Aleppo once, where an evil, dishonorable Turk beat a Venetian and insulted the state, I took the circumcised dog by the throat and killed him like this. [Stabs himself]

LODOVICO: *Oh, bloody end!*

GRATIANO: *All that is said is ruined.*

OTHELLO: *I kissed you before I killed you. There is no other way for me to go than to kill myself and die on a kiss.* [Falls on the bed, and dies]

CASSIO: *I was afraid he would do this because of his great courage, but I did not think he had a weapon.*

LODOVICO: [To Iago] *Oh, cold-hearted dog, this pain was more fatal than hunger on the sea! Look at the tragic pile on this bed. You have done this, and it makes me sick. Cover them. Gratiano, stay in this house and take what the Moor owns because you are his heir. To you, Lord Governor Cassio, is left the job of punishing this hellish villain Iago. The time, the place, and the torture are yours to enforce. I will return to Venice with a sorrowful heart and relate this sorrowful event to the state.*

[Exeunt]

267

Study Guide

Act I, Scene 1

1. From Roderigo's first speech it appears that he paid Iago for something. Can you tell what it was? Iago says he hates Othello. For what reason?

2. What two kinds of followers are there, according to Iago? Shortly after this, Iago speaks to the point of appearance and reality. He concludes, "I am not what I am." State what precedes and explain this line.

3. How do Iago and Roderigo stir up trouble?
   What is Brabantio's reaction?

Act I, Scene 2

1. Why does Iago say he wishes to kill Roderigo? What reason does Iago give for not killing Roderigo? What is Othello's response? Why is Othello not worried about Brabantio's wrath?

2. What message does Cassio bring? As Othello is about to leave for the Senate, Brabantio and his supporters show up and draw their swords. How would you describe Othello when he responds?

3. Brabantio wishes to arrest Othello and hold him in jail until he can be brought to court. What does Brabantio accuse Othello of? What forces Brabantio to change his plans?

Act I, Scene 3

1. As at the opening of scenes 1 and 2 the audience is smack in the middle of the action. About what are the Duke and Senators concerned?

2. By what adjective do the Senators and the Duke refer to Othello? What does this indicate?

3. How does the Senate react to Brabantio's charges against Othello? What does the Duke say? What is the tone of Othello's response to this? What does this say about his temperament?

4. Othello tells us how he won Desdemona's heart. How did he do this?

5. Desdemona speaks well before the group, and Brabantio is convinced she did it of her own free will. The Duke then gives Brabantio advice. What is Brabantio's mood at this point?

6. Everyone has left and Roderigo tells Iago he is going to drown himself. What is Iago's response? What is Iago's view of human nature? Of love?

7. After Roderigo leaves we see into Iago's thoughts in his soliloquy. What is his opinion of Roderigo? Why does he hate the Moor? What plan has he formulated?

Act II, Scene 1

1. What news do we get of the Turkish fleet? On the dock, we see that Iago's fierce mood has not abated. What does he observe, and what does he conclude?

2. It is clear that Iago views Othello as "different" and thinks that eventually Desdemona will, too. Why does he think Desdemona will lose her love for Othello?

3. In Iago's soliloquy at the end of this scene we again see into his mind and, unlike dialogue, he has no reason to lie. What does he believe about Cassio and Desdemona? Of Othello and Desdemona? His own feelings for Desdemona? His suspicions of the Moor? How does he plan to discredit Cassio?

Act II, Scene 3

1. What is Othello's opinion of Iago? Why is Cassio reluctant to have a drink? Why does he finally agree? How does the clever Iago in one breath praise and condemn Cassio to Montano?

2. After not getting a straight answer from anyone, Othello says, "My blood begins my safer guides to rule, and passion, having by best judgment collided, assays to lead the way." What is his point and what does he threaten? How is this a departure from his earlier temperament, and what makes it ominous?

3. Reluctantly, Iago tells Othello what happened. How is Othello's reaction all that Iago had hoped for? What advice does Iago give Cassio?

4. Once again, Iago's soliloquy gives us a glimpse into his plans. He concludes, "So will I turn her virtue into pitch, and out of her own goodness make the net that shall enmesh them all." What is he saying, and how does he plan to accomplish this?

Act III, Scene 1
1. Why does Cassio pay money to the clown to find Emilia? What does Emilia tell Cassio? How could Cassio upset Iago's plan?

Act III, Scene 2 & Scene 3
1. Is Emilia part of Iago's plot, or does she truly believe that Iago is saddened by what happened to Cassio?

2. For what two reasons does Desdemona agree to plead Cassio's case?

3. Desdemona pleads Cassio's case, and Othello agrees to reinstate him. What happens next?

4. What does Iago say about the women of Venice? Why might Othello be inclined to believe this?

5. Desdemona's handkerchief becomes an important piece of stage business. Why does Desdemona produce it? What happens to it? What does Emilia plan to do with it? Finally, who gets it, and what is to be done with it?

6. What further proof of Desdemona's disloyalty does Iago give Othello?

Act III, Scene 4

1. Why does Desdemona not wish to admit to Othello that she lost the handkerchief? Why does he demand to see it?

2. What does Desdemona think is the cause of Othello's anger? What point does Emilia raise?

Act IV, Scene 1

1. Iago agitates Othello with lewd images. What is the result? How does Iago say he'll show Othello further proof?

2. How does Iago manage to get Cassio to talk about Bianca while Othello thinks he is talking about Desdemona?

3. Why does Othello say of Desdemona one moment that she is a sweet creature and, in another breath, talk of letting her rot?

4. What news does Lodovico bring from Venice?
    After Othello slaps Desdemona in front of the guests, how does she react?

5. In his somewhat deranged state, Othello refers to goats and monkeys. It appears to make no sense, but the audience knows that it is a reference to what earlier comments in the play by Iago?

Act IV, Scene 2

1. Othello tells Emilia to guard the door as a madame in a brothel might. What is his frame of mind?

2. What does Emilia say is the reason for Othello's jealousy? What is Iago's reaction to this?

3. Roderigo shows up. What is his complaint? How does Iago win Roderigo back to his side?

Act IV, Scene 3

1. Having made up his mind, Othello seems much calmer now. What is revealed about Desdemona's thoughts?

2. Desdemona has been abused, slapped and humiliated by her husband, yet she loves him and hopes to convince him of this. Does she seem weak or foolish because of this?

Act V, Scene 1
1. For what reasons does Iago want Cassio dead? How can Iago benefit from Roderigo's death?

2. What saves Cassio? Why does Roderigo say to Iago, "O dammed Iago! O inhuman dog!"

Act V, Scene 2
1. Why does Othello say, "No heaven forfend! I would not kill thy soul?"

2. As Desdemona tries to convince Othello that she is innocent of what he accuses her, she breaks down and weeps at what news? How does Othello interpret her weeping?

3. Why does Emilia repeat the phrase, "My husband," three times? At this point, why does Othello draw his sword on Emilia?

4. Iago tells Emilia to go home, but she refuses. Why is he telling her to leave, and why does she refuse?

5. What is Othello's request of Lodovico? Othello kills himself, and Lodovico and Gratiano prepare to return to Venice. What will be the future for Cassio and Iago?